Manage This Lead That

A Practical Look at Leadership and You!

John T. Majoy

J T M

TABLE OF CONTENTS

WHAT TYPE OF LEADER ARE YOU?

Welcome to the wild world of leadership! Good leaders are invited to their retirement party, not excluded.

Before you get into the meat and potatoes of this book all readers should take note of what you are about to experience. A key to a successful book or essay is whether it captures the reader's attention. There are boat loads of books on leadership, so why choose this one? The answer is easy: leaders need to educate themselves and one way of accomplishing this is to learn from others. I am not the end-all solution to solve all your leadership issues nor do I promise to bring resolve to the challenges of being a leader. Rather, I will share many perspectives that you may be able to apply into your leadership style and elevate your thinking on issues relating to leadership.

As we begin, it may help to identify what type of leader you are. There is the autocratic leader who essentially is a ruler who has control over everything. Good, bad, or otherwise, there are places in the world for this type of leader. The leader of this type may be referred to as a micro-manager or perhaps obsessive compulsive. Adding or combining a narcissist into this style of leadership would be like taking a cookie sheet, filling it full of gasoline and then lighting it on fire, which I do not recommend trying. In other words, it will be a decent size fire, hot as hell, enough to burn you, and a fire that spreads when you go to put it out. As we will discuss further in this book, leaders should be putting out fires, not spreading them. Without question, the narcissist will not be invited to his/her retirement party, something we will also talk about later.

A democratic leader is simply one who takes input from others and uses this to make decisions. Not a bad style to speak of, but this leader could also have issues as it relates to the inability to make a command decision. On the flip side, others within the organization may feel valued, appreciated, and worthy. There is strength in numbers and a combined effort can aid any organization to greatness. While no there are no guarantees in life, the democratic leader will likely be invited to his/her retirement party.

Laisses-faire leaders are your best friends. These folks essentially let others do as they please and are the opposite of the micromanager. Such is not necessarily a bad thing because if there is a room full of quality leaders, the head cheese would be smart to let them do their thing. To the contrary, this type of leader may be the one who is too worried about being friends with their employees versus being their leader. They may also want to avoid the challenges that go with being a leader. Like an ostrich with its head in the sand, this leader may not see things that are happening around them. This type of leader will be invited to his/her retirement party. In fact, they'll probably plan it themselves.

Yes, there are other types of leadership styles out there but let's use these three as a baseline to build from. I do not think there is a perfect description that can encompass the perfect leader because one does not exist. Rather, like tools in the toolchest, the best leaders are the ones who use the best tools to get the job done. An analogy I enjoy using relates to perhaps my least favorite baseball team, the New York Yankees. However, giving credit due is proper and it goes like this: The Yankees coach Joe Torre won four World Series titles. He did not win these by putting his friends in to pitch, pinch hit or run, or play any of the field positions. Rather, he put the best players in the best places at the best times which brought him these championships. He staffed his team with the best of the best players and positioned them well. Yes, the deep pockets funding these players helped, of course. However, the analogy remains the same: put the right people in the right places at peak performance levels and it will pay dividends.

I will share many of my analogies and hopefully this will help put things into perspective for you. During this book, you will find places where I may repeat myself or word things differently. I tried not to step on any toes or offend anyone but in today's world that is hard. Regardless, I hope you will gain some new insights, elevate your thinking, and perhaps have a better mindset toward being a leader. Whether you are a current leader, up and coming leader, or one whose eyes are on a future leadership position, this book is for you.

What type of leader are you? Why do you want to be a leader? How can you become a better leader?

Well, read on and let's get you those answers.

PS: I am a Cleveland Indians (Guardians) fan, true and true, sorry Yankee fans.

THE BOSSHOLE

T he best way to start out a book on leadership is to define the type of leader you do not want to be. Since 2011 I have taught leadership courses for first line supervisors, mid-level managers and law enforcement executives. I use a few analogies to try to get my points across to them in hopes of making them a better leader. One exercise I do is to ask members of the class to raise their hands if they have ever worked for a bad leader. In all my years and over a thousand students, there was only one who did not raise a hand. In statistics we call this an outlier. In the real world we call this someone with little life experience.

Being that 99.999% of the students raised their hands, it sends a clear message: there are some bad leaders out there, and not everyone is cut out to be a leader. Such does not make them bad people as we all put our shoes on the same way. I commend those who can recognize they are not leaders as this is a strength they have. It is those who relish becoming a leader for the wrong reasons that scares me. Or, worse yet, those who are clearly not suited to be a leader but somehow weasel their way into such a position. Which leads us to the next type of leader: the bosshole.

I am unsure of the origin of this word, but this is simply a combination between a boss and an asshole. The leader fitting this description is one who does not value people for their worth. Rather, keeping it real, this leader is an asshole. The critical infrastructure of any organization is its people, regardless of the nature of the business, you will hear me repeat this again. People make the world go around and often leaders lose sight of their biggest asset. I get it, people can also be assholes and I've had my turn at being one and working with them. This bodes to the statement (another analogy), "Life is easy, people make it hard." However, just because people are assholes does not mean you should be one too. It is much harder to be a leader than it is to be an asshole. In fact, being an asshole comes quite easy, but ask yourself this question: do you want to work for an asshole? The fear of becoming one should be enough; after all, misery loves company.

I always wonder when I see promotions to leadership positions of those who should not be there. In a joking sense, these can be the people who got their asses kicked when they were young, and they need to get back at the world. Kidding, of course, but think about the origin of the bosshole. Could this be from drinking the cool-aid, which we will talk about later. Or could this be a personality trait that they have to boss people around and tell them every move to make. This is the kind of person whose iron fist leadership or lead by coercion is optimal for them. They have a grudge, and treating people like crap is their goal of proving their self-worth. Trust me, I've worked with one; well, several, but one takes the crown. Unbeknownst to him, I share my experiences often with my students. Not by name of course, because he doesn't deserve the credit, but rather how I never wanted to be like him in this lifetime or any others. We will talk about him soon.

The micromanager could potentially fit this role of being a bosshole for many reasons. The bosshole has his/her fingers in everything and people need to ask permission to do just about everything. The people working for the bosshole are generally wound tight, fragile, and afraid to make a decision. They may appear to be happy but inside they are stressed, insecure and feel underappreciated. When they go home, odds are their misery carries over to their home life, which is not cool.

The bosshole is also one who has friends on demand. In other words, folks probably do not like him/her, but they must because it's the boss. These are the kinds of people who may run into the bosshole when he/she stops walking. Or, like the puppy dog who just took a beating for chewing up your dress shoes but five minutes later he/she is sitting on your lap or licking your feet. The friends (again) drink the cool-aid and will work to fit the square peg into the round hole knowing full well it does not belong there. They will do so because the boss wants them to, or they want to impress the boss. The problem is that impressing the boss will fly about as far as a lead balloon.

A bosshole could also capitalize on their "friends" in the organization where they will use them to complete certain tasks that are less than desirable. The followers will go along with the bosshole even though deep down inside their gut is telling them this is contrary to their principles. The fear of being ostracized by the bosshole will get others to comply with their motivations. Such actions may include disciplining or unfairly treating those who are not in the "good ole boys club" or any outsider who will not drink the cool-aid. Yes, I call it "cool-aid" knowing the drink I am referring to is "Kool Aid." But, as an analogy, these folks also want to be "cool" in the eyes of the bosshole.

Can you imagine a backyard barbecue at the bosshole's house? Wouldn't I like to be a fly on the wall there. I vision the bosshole telling the dumbest jokes and all the followers laughing like hyenas and rolling on the floor. The followers will compliment the food even though it tastes like it was scooped out of a dumpster. The followers may bring a nice bottle of wine or bourbon as a token of appreciation to the bosshole for being a bosshole. This then leads us to the next phase of the bosshole era.

There are also up-and-coming bossholes that thrive on the leader's action and want to be just like him or her. They will do things to please the bosshole which includes treating others like crap or looking for reasons to throw others under the bus to cloud their own transgressions or insecurities. These individuals are generally not too popular within the rank and file, obviously. However, they may also put on a good facade where others may want to follow in their shoes. The vulnerable ones may buy into this, but the best advice is to watch out for the wolves in sheep clothing as this is a commonality.

If you see an up-and-coming bosshole, you would be doing them a great service to bring them back to planet earth. Sometimes this could be too late, like a house fire that is totally engulfed where the firemen get out the marshmallows and wienies and watch it burn because it is too far gone to save. However, for those who can be saved, give them my one piece of free leadership advice: do not forget where you came from. I'll mention this several times in this book because I feel it is important to emphasize.

By the way, have you ever heard of a good ole boys club? Of course, you have. Are you in one? Are you on the outside looking in? Or do you have your head up someone else's butt that does not allow you to see clearly? If you have ever been on the outside looking in, this is not a fun position to be in. The results can cause future leaders to lose interest or draw resentment because their boss is an asshole, plays favorites and enjoys the company of a save ass, suck ass and kiss ass (yes, another analogy). Seeing through this is not terribly difficult, overcoming it may be.

The solution is very simple. First, do not join the good ole boys club. Or, make everyone in the organization a part of the club. Or, better yet, make sure one does not exist. If you are transitioning into the role of a leader, see through this and dissolve this club forever. If there are those club members that resent your transition as they enjoy being in the club, simply tell them this: the bus is at the bus stop and there is a seat for everyone. Jump on board and let's go for a ride. Sounds good, right? It will only be as good as those who get on the bus by choice and want to go for a ride, versus those who get on the bus in a negative fashion. If they do not want to get on the bus, they can take a hike. Not to be viewed negatively but sometimes there is addition through subtraction. The future bossholes need to get on board and transition or they need to take their talents and negativity somewhere else.

When I became a police chief I came in from the outside. No friends, family, or people whom I knew. I was a stranger to them as they were to me. I did not reside in the community, nor did I know any of the residents, business owners or other stakeholders. When I first met the members of the department, I could feel there was a lot of anxiety in the room. Some seemed relieved to see me, others had already decided they didn't like me, and some rode the fence to see what was going to happen. It did not take too long to see who was willing to get on the bus. Subconsciously some tested me in different fashions to see what they could get away with. They treaded lightly because they did not want to overstep their boundaries. I was not too worried because it is mostly a common reaction. I did learn how there were those who wanted to form a coup against me for some reason. I am guessing because I brought the word "accountable" with me which was foreign to some. The police officers were not setting a good example by their arbitrary enforcement of the law. Tickets were being written for petty things and cars towed simply because their license plates had been expired for 24-48 hours. There were more wrongdoings, but I will not bore you with them. Ultimately, it was not good policing in my opinion.

My first vow was not to make any major changes for 90 days having read a book about that. This lasted about three days before I saw things that did not bode to my style of policing and leadership. I implemented a new daily activity report for officers to complete. This was moreover a reminder of the tasks they were directed to complete during their tour of duty. Not so long thereafter, there was a use of force incident that somehow made the local news, essentially ostracizing the officer one-sidedly. In the reporter's hand was one of our daily activity reports that had recently been implemented. I had no public records requests for these nor did any go outside of the department to my knowledge. However, I quickly learned there were a few that disliked the word accountability and wanted to see me fail. They figured that by calling the "news" (loosely defined) that a negative story would make me look bad. Sad for them I didn't give a shit. Unfortunately for them it was a futile attempt, and myself and those with me could see right through them. On a good note, those who attempted the coup failed and left on their own because they decided not to get on the bus.

From this experience I learned the leaders before me had somewhat of a combination of a laisse faire style of leader and an autocratic leader. This is rare but essentially it allowed some of the police officers to do whatever they wanted, and others were reprimanded for a farting upwind, well not really but you get the point. I learned there was a good old boys club and those who were not in it got the short end of the stick. In fact, about a month after the former chief left, he was still trying to get one of the good officers fired because he didn't like him. Who does this, you ask. Well, the short answer is a poor leader.

Within the police department there was little accountability and the city administration did not trust the police department, deservingly so. Fortunately for me the administration stayed open minded and saw through the past transgressions of the prior regimes and allowed me to do my thing. Again, I was not the answer to everything holy but as a department we advanced ourselves to gain the trust of the administration and community. In doing so, I strived every day not to be a bosshole, having worked for one myself. I'm sure there were times where I may have been called one, but I really tried hard not to be one.

Have you worked for a bosshole? I have and odds are you have. My bosshole story is one who there was no pleasing. No matter what was done it was not enough. For example, "You did a good job, but..." How many times have you heard that? The bosshole always has a better idea, knows pretty much everything, and does not want to see anyone with more success than them.

The expected outcome of working for a bosshole is increased stress, for starters. It can also lower productivity, morale, and lessen the overall wellbeing of the organization. In my situation, the bosshole would go on screaming rants, throw a fit over the most minor and mundane things along with keeping things real with the good ole boys club. There were people so far up the ass of the bosshole that it made it hard to discern one from another. At a young age I discovered workplace stress resulting from the bosshole. I was filled with resentment because it got old trying to give 100% and do a good job while being shot down when I did. I often felt that I could come up with a wage-doubling opportunity only to have it be shot down. I could make a bunch of arrests, apprehend violent criminals, and sustain high levels of productivity, only to get the "good job, but" speech. I really should call this the "butt" speech because that is essentially where I wanted him to shove it.

I have no regrets about working for a bosshole because it allowed me to develop myself into the leader I wanted to be, which was certainly not like that. On a favorable note, I had a leader who was in favor of training his people. As such, I had the good fortune of attending leadership schools, seminars and various training events and appreciate that which I learned from all of them. However, I likely learned more from working for bad leaders than I ever did in any of the training I received. Such is not to diminish leadership training as it is an important component of any successful leader. However, what does this equate to, you may ask? The answer is simple, be the leader you want to be, do not mirror someone else. You may like traits from some of the leaders you have encountered in your life, use them! The same can be said about the bad traits, avoid them. Regardless, you should take all the tools in the toolchest and compile them into the best leadership you can offer. Sounds easy right? As my high school football coach would tell us, wish in one hand and shit in another, which weighs more? You'll hear this again.

Let's read on...

THE LITMUS TEST

Leaders need to be well-versed in the daily operations of the organization, which goes without saying. A Litmus test is essentially one that is a decisive test. The test has a real outcome that is validated and sustained. How does this apply to leadership? It is simple, as a leader you will be tested, and you will test others. Subordinate personnel will subconsciously test you to see how far they can go, or how much they can get away with. The leader needs to be able to recognize these individuals and keep them in check. Do not look at this as a bad thing as it a generally a natural progression. It is smart to value your people, but keep in mind that the leader somehow needs to make unpopular decisions for the betterment of the organization.

As a leader you will also use the litmus test. The key to the success of this test is to remain open minded that the decision may be fluid. A leader makes mistakes just like everyone else. They use logic and cognitive processes to help make key decisions. You will test your people subconsciously, which is also not a bad thing. As in the Joe Torre analogy, you must get the right people on board and hopefully those will come from within. A good leader cannot do everything

MANAGE THIS LEAD THAT   13

for himself/herself. Rather, it takes a team of quality leaders to band together toward accomplishing the goals of the organization. Torre put the best of the best together and they won the World Series. As a leader, you can do the same thing. You may not win the World Series but you will be able to accomplish many things by having your team work together.

As a test, a good leader should evaluate the effectiveness of his/her workforce. Are we doing a good job? Where can we improve? Can we streamline processes where it will help the organization go from good to great?

If you are starting off as a new leader you will certainly need to use the Litmus test, and often. Developing a baseline of trust and confidence with your people will be impactful. If you want to look at it otherwise, imagine a leader who does not develop trust and confidence. This could be the making of a bosshole right before your very eyes.

During my career in law enforcement, I spent five years on a special response team. We trained heavily in weapons, tactics, room clearing and more. I was a young vibrant officer and enjoyed almost every minute of it. My one exception was during a major training event where our team leader was not there and the second in command was in charge. While mostly a decent guy, he was not the best leader. He was on his way to being a bosshole but failed at it, which should speak volumes as the next thing higher than a bosshole is a flaming effing asshole. In this instance he made it known that he was in charge of the team. The rest of the team didn't really give a shit because he was like the substitute teacher for the seventh-grade science class where students simply just didn't care. Herein, we were doing room clearing drills and his orders were to enter in a particular way, spread out and clear the room. The team was left scratching its head and several of us, me included, expressed our concern that this was not the best way and that we had not done things this way before. Rather than considering the thought of the team, the acting team leader dug his heels in, and we did it his way. After we ran things his way, the instructors of the course reamed us a new asshole as our tactics were completely unsafe and could get someone killed.

Despite being wrong, the leader defended his actions and continued to dig in his heels. The rest of team just held their heads and remained silent while he was doing an outstanding job of getting his lunch handed to him. I was quietly laughing inside as I was thinking to myself, you will later become a failed bosshole, and fast forward a handful of years later, I discovered I was right. Make no mistake, I've been wrong in many, many, cases but in this one I nailed it.

What is the takeaway you ask? There are several. First, leaders using the Litmus Test must be open minded. If you make a decision and do not stick to it, you are not a failure. Rather, you are a leader. If you make a wrong decision, dig in your heels, and refuse to change it, you may not be a great leader. You may look at this as a sign of weakness, instability or being wishy-washy. You may feel others will look differently at you because you changed your mind. You may feel it is best to stick with your decision and defend it at all costs. Or, in other words, you did not use the Litmus Test but rather are working very hard at fitting the square peg into the round hole. While you may ultimately be successful fitting the peg into the round hole, it is not designed to be there. Your decision may bode well now, but not in a long-term sense. In sum, a quality leader is open minded, realizes he/she may not always be right, or their decisions may not be the best at the time. How one acts in a situation like this can be a true definition of their leadership character.

Are you afraid to make a mistake? Do you dig in your heels and etch things in stone when you may not be right? Do you defend yourself even though you know you are wrong?

Being a leader requires the individual to be courageous and able to make critical decisions that can impact an organization. Leaders should not be weak nor show signs of weakness, right? Well, let's talk about that. Show me someone without a weakness and I will sell you a bridge. We all have weaknesses, we all procrastinate, we all have a boiling point, we are all human. One of the first things a leader should recognize is that they are human. We are imperfect, flawed and make mistakes. This mindset can help keep leaders grounded. Of course, we want to be strong, and we must be. But that does not mean we cannot use a weakness as a strength.

Going back to the special response team incident. The temporary team leader could have easily changed the dynamic of the entire situation. His personality would not allow him to do so, despite everyone else trying to get him to do it. To turn the situation around, he could have simply admitted that his decision was not best practice and remained open minded to adapt and overcome. He could have asked for examples or a demonstration to better his abilities and that of the team. He could have said that he should have followed the advice of his team and asked for another opportunity to complete the exercise. All of these would have gained him a lot of capital with the instructors, the team, and other teams. Unfortunately, that did not happen. Other teams looked at our team a little differently but mostly him because they collaboratively agreed they were glad he was not their leader.

As I noted earlier, life is easy, people make it hard. This individual leader was one who should not have been in that position. As a special response team operator, he was good. His shooting skills and operational tactics were spot on as a team member. However, when you put him in charge of people, things turned to shit fast. This shows that not everyone is cut out to be a leader. This does not make them a bad person, bad employee, or dreg of society. There are some police officers who complete a 25-year career – or more – and do not seek promotion or advancement. Some may think less of them. However, the reality is commendable as the individual made a smart decision and understood their calling was not in a leadership position. There is nothing wrong with this and it is rather noble. The problem is that there are not too many of these folks around who recognize this. Rather, some thrive to be in that leadership position for the wrong reasons. Yes, you may get paid more. Yes, you may receive recognition or become popular among others. Yes, as in policing, you may get the stars and gold badge. The reality is that it can be lonely at the top. We've all heard the statement how shit slides downhill. While mostly true, look at situations where leaders have failed because the shit slid uphill.

We can look at leaders who have been forced to step down, or perhaps voluntarily doing so when the organization fails. Take a professional sports team, like my favorite Cleveland Browns, a couple losing seasons is likely going to get you a trip to the general manager's office where you will get your walking papers. Despite giving it your all, the team failed so you're done. In my life there have been many instances where leaders have had to step aside for one reason or another. Mostly (and probably in many cases) it is where the organization has failed. Large or small, the success of the organization falls upon its leadership. In sum, shit does slide uphill.

How do we slow down the shit from sliding uphill you may ask? The answer can be delineated in several ways. First, let's look back to the Joe Torre example. He was able to get the right people on board. As a leader, it is important to get the right people on board. It is important to be careful not to get bosshole wannabes. In other words, there are people who are up your butt and fall into the category as a save ass, suck ass, or kiss ass. As the leader it is not all too difficult to get others to agree with you. But the hard part is getting the people you want, and they are those who are willing to disagree with you. Disagreement can be synonymous with progress.

Think about this for a minute. There are a lot of people out there who agree simply because it is easy, may score them points, or because they are afraid to disagree. The situation is known as the Abilene Paradox. In this situation, a family of four, mom, dad, son, and daughter, all agree to drive 50 miles to Abilene, Texas, to get cafeteria food. The drive was long, hot and the food was awful. On the ride home, everyone blamed one another for agreeing to travel this route when the reality was that everyone agreed for different reasons. The outcome was everyone was pissed at one another, and it was a colossal waste of time. No one spoke up and said it was a bad idea because they didn't want to upset anyone. They didn't want to challenge the status-quo or risk someone getting butthurt because they didn't go along with the idea. In sum, they disagree, and they all suffered the consequences of not dissenting. Your team needs to learn this.

To the contrary, there are some who disagree on purpose just to be an asshole. The person in this category is a professional jackass whose goal is to be a professional jackass, mission accomplished. The dissent to a majority empowers them, makes them feel special despite everyone in the room silently calling them an asshole below their breath.

Before you ask, yes, I have worked with an individual like this. Their modus operandi was to simply be a professional jackass. The "I'm gonna fight you on that one" mindset. The person will fight a decision despite it having no impact upon them whatsoever. They will bitch, piss and moan about mundane things and like a communicable disease, their venom can easily be spread to other teammates. Most susceptible to this are those younger or less experienced individuals who can fall prey to this person. They idolize this person because they stand up to the administration, or so they think. They may think this person has cajónes the size of watermelons and the strength of a giant. The truth is individuals like this are harmful to an organization. I am not saying one cannot disagree because I emphasize that disagreement can mean progress. This is a different type of disagreement. This type of disagreement is one that diffuses innovation, stalls projects and turns a 30 minute meeting to a 90 minute meeting because they want to argue because they just want to enhance their professional jackass portfolio.

The example I must share was with a drug raid that our special response team was about to embark upon. Planning a dynamic raid is important and there are many variables to consider. Our team leader was always very well prepared, organized and three steps ahead of everyone else. That is what a good team leader does. However, during the pre-raid briefing, despite hours and hours of detailed planning having been made, reviewed, and agreed upon, the professional jackass decided to raise his hand and start questioning everything. The rest of us wanted to take out a rubber hose and smack him upside the head (joking, but not) because we all thought the plan was well suited, detailed and, most importantly, safe. The pre-raid briefing took twice the amount of time it should have simply because the team leader had to defend his plan and answer a host of questions that were irrelevant. There was another team assisting us on this raid, so I was not clear if he was trying to impress others or just showing how much of a jackass he really was. Regardless, he accomplished his mission of pissing everyone off. Ultimately the raid went off as planned, we arrested the bad guy, no one was hurt, and we seized a boat load of dope. Funny, in the after-raid debriefing, he said very little, thereby showing how much of a jackass he really was.

The next big question is how to deal with a person like this. I have a simple answer. It may not be popular, may not win your points or get you Christmas cards, but it is the right way. All too often we hear people say, "Oh, that's Tom, he's always been that way." They are speaking in terms of him being a professional jackass. My response is simple, "Tom is that way because no one called him on his shit." In other words, sometimes people must be called out. Is there a perfect way? No, there is not. However, there are tools in the toolchest to use. The first may be a nicey-nicey approach. Take the drug raid briefing, the police chief may nicely call out the member without embarrassing them. However, while seemingly harmless, it may not be all too effective. The next step is to completely shut them down, again, nicely to the best degree possible. If that does not work, then you may have to resort to putting your foot down, but not up their ass. Call them on their shit in front of other people and maybe, just maybe, they'll get the hint. As a last resort, you may have to call them in and give them the bad news that they are not developing nor helping, and it is time to make a change. Going back to there is a seat on the bus, get on and take a ride. Do not be a professional jackass.

You see, as humans we are creatures of habit, some good, some not. We are imperfect beings and make mistakes. Sometimes we need to be called out; have our wings clipped, our lunch handed to us, or perhaps a good old-fashioned ass chewing. Keeping it positive is paramount because we cannot lose sight that our people are our critical infrastructure. Part of being a leader is developing other leaders. By calling out others on their shit may not be popular at the time, but perhaps the individual will thank you later, or their co-worker will! Or, perhaps you were on the receiving end of this where it ended making you a better leader. A key ingredient to this will be to watch how the individual reacts. If they are open-minded, adapting and accepting, this treatment is a good thing. If they are resentful and do not change their ways, this wishy-washy, it is a bad thing. Again, always try to keep things positive when talking to your people. Remember, the tail does not wag the dog. But, it is a happy dog whose tail wags.

As leaders, if we could wave a magic wand and fix things we would. No one said that leadership is easy. We have learned that shit slides uphill, the square peg belongs in the square hole, people need to be called on their shit, and we need to remain open minded when doing the Litmus Test of leadership.

Let's read on...

SQUARE PEG, ROUND HOLE

T here are no shortcuts to any place worth going. As discussed, no one will tell you being in a leadership role is easy. They will not tell you the road will be smooth and free of bumps because it will not be. Rather, it can be awfully lonely at the top. These statements are not meant to deter you from reaching the top as this could be no further from the truth. It is meant to prepare you to get to the top and reach the success you have worked for.

When you are in a leadership role you will face an ethical decision every day. This is not just five days a week but rather seven days a week, 365 days out of the year. A series of bad decisions only leads to worse decisions. We all make mistakes and if we could do things differently in life perhaps, we would. This chapter is about preparing you to make the tough decisions and appreciating the value in those decisions you make.

When a leader is tasked with a tough decision, some may elect to take the route of least resistance. While seemingly easy and time saving, the long-term repercussions will be bad. At present, you may not think of the long-term challenges that will arise because you rushed, hurried, and took the easy way to get it done. This is where the square peg and round hole analogy kicks in. If you find yourself in a situation where you are trying to make the square peg fit into the round hole, it is time to step back and reevaluate.

I enjoy reading books about leadership and talking to others about what they have learned. I also enjoy interacting with other leaders and future leaders because there is much to learn from them. One thing I have learned is that we have all been guilty to some degree of trying to fit the square peg into the round hole. Some have had bad consequences, some only mild, but the opportunity to learn from this is the key to becoming a better leader.

This chapter is purely about the square peg/round hole analogy. The key here is to recognize this before it happens. Taking the path of least resistance is easy, without controversy and may make most happy. As a leader, does your job description include making people happy? Such is not to say we should not try to keep our people happy because good leaders will always want to do that. Good leaders also recognize this may not always be possible. The way it is dealt with may weigh heavily upon our people. There is one thing that everyone in the world wants, and it is free to give out: respect. When you respect your people, they will respect you. Even if there are times when you must make tough decisions that may impact your people, do it respectfully. Yes, I get it, this is much easier said than done. Before making that critical decision or delivering the news, put some thought into it. We have all seen knee-jerk reactions and the tertiary effect of these upon our people. The impact is harmful to the organization, and it is like a breach of the bridge of trust, and this is very hard to rebuild.

While I have many examples of the square peg/round hole theory, I'm quite certain you may also have the same. The reality is that we are all guilty to some degree of trying to make things work despite knowing full well that they are not designed as such. The one classic example that comes to mind is a situation where a young police officer was steadfast on his plight to make an arrest on a burglary suspect. The challenge was that there was just not enough evidence to make a case. He knew who the culprit was, and all roads were leading to a specific suspect. However, because of a lack of physical evidence we were not able to secure an indictment. The officer had a difficult time with this and understandably so. When I spoke with the officer, I sensed his frustration, and I asked him one simple question: did you turn over every stone possible to make this case? The answer was a yes. I then told the officer that he had done everything possible to solve the case. Could the officer have tried to fit the square peg into the round hole but cutting corners or taking shortcuts? Absolutely. But, to compromise one's integrity or reputation is not something worth considering. Hence the analogy of the square peg in the round hole. Cases like this are not uncommon and it's not letting the bad guy get away scot-free, rather, it is realizing that you've done your best and sometimes that is all one can ask for.

As leaders our days are full of meetings, paperwork, administrative functions and, if we are lucky, some proactive means to take the organization to the next level. It would come easy to take shortcuts to save time, effort, and energy. As I noted in the first paragraph of this chapter, there are no shortcuts to any place worth going. It is easy to take the path of least resistance and shrug things off haphazardly to get them done. Leaders cannot always function this way because it may provide temporary reasoning and save time, but the long-term repercussions will have a substantial impact on the organization.

We are a society today of get rich quick schemes, people who want to have the world handed to them on a silver platter and not have to work toward their goals. We will discuss this later when we speak of

Generation WTF. For now, we need to understand that there are no shortcuts to any place worth going but also how to forge a path to get there.

I encountered a sharable situation where the square peg was put into the round hole. Once again, it's a police-related story. The powers that be came up with a brilliant idea to combine the police and fire departments together and form one public safety department. Sounds good, right? Think of it: the policemen become firemen and the firemen become policemen. We are all public servants, why not combine the two? Makes sense (not).

As a part of this conceptual idea, it cost over $25,000 which may not sound like a lot of money for a very large organization. However, it was not a very large organization, and that money could have been spent in a better way. I think you can see where this is going. I worked with a young police officer who had this grandiose idea that he was going to quit police work and sell boats. He bragged about how much money he was going to make and all the free time he would have. No more nights, weekends and holidays worked. Yay him! Unfortunately, the bad news was that if we could all make millions of dollars selling boats, we'd all be selling boats. Make no mistake, there are some who do and have, but not as many as you'd think. The analogy here is simple, if combining police and fire together was such a brilliant idea, then why was no one else doing it? Why were we being the Guinee pigs?

We spent hours and hours of gathering calls for service data and the time officers were spending on various tasks of their respective shifts. They took two months of data: February and August and were able to somehow use a Ph.D. to state that the police officers had plenty of time on their hands to respond to EMS and fire calls. The same applied to the firemen as they too had plenty of time to do their jobs and add some policing to it. The concept of combining the two departments together is not new and, in fact, there are some that are doing it already. However, in Ohio, there were a grand total of two cities or villages that were doing it. Again, if it was such a good thing, why wasn't everyone doing it?

The writing on the wall was clear, the cops didn't want to be firemen and the firemen didn't want to be cops. How hard is that? Well, when you make them transition, their hands will be held out seeking more pay. The police officer must now be a paramedic and firefighter, then pay me. The fireman must go to the police academy and to this on top of being a fireman, then pay me. The jobs of police officers and firefighters are complex and require a lot of training up front but ongoing training. The concept is not a horrible one, but there would have been a lot of unhappy employees should this have been forced upon us.

Somehow the leader was able to convince elected officials to spend the money on the concept. At the end of the day, it was a colossal waste of time and money. What happened? Nothing. We spent so much time and effort on this initiative, all for naught. The $25k price tag does not equate to the stressors and impact it had on personnel, let alone the time spent on it. Some personnel considered leaving for other jobs, but their kids were in the local schools, or their spouses had local jobs. Talk about adding unneeded stress! The upper echelon did not seem to care.

When all the dust settled and the smoke cleared, it was clear that the square peg of combining police and fire departments was not going to fit into the round hole of saving money and better services, period. The leader never took accountability for this failure but rather explained that it was a necessary study to try and save money for the city. Well, clearly it did not. Before embarking on such a journey, would it not be smart to seek input from your department leaders?

You should trust their years of service and depth of knowledge. The answer was a clear no, such was not the case. To their credit, the department leaders were open-minded to the concept, knowing full well in the backs of their mind that it would never happen. They were right.

The moral of the story has several dimensions. First, this did not pass the Litmus Test. Second, the leader did not consult the leadership team, that being the police and fire chiefs, but rather looked at a potential accolade for himself by using the "look what I did" syndrome. Next, it was a clear-cut example of how the square peg does not fit into the round hole. For clarity, there were good leaders in this instance, but their decisions were less than good and I'm being kind to this end. I am glad it had a good ending but it really took some time for people to overcome the unnecessary challenges this brought upon the organization.

Leaders need to try and save money for the organization, that is understood. But there is also the cost of doing business. The fat can be trimmed in many places and a little here and there can add up. However, where we need to be careful is the impact on the organization and its critical infrastructure, the people. Have you ever run into someone who does nothing but complain about their job? I'm guessing you have because there are plenty. Have you ever asked them why they hate their jobs so much? You will probably receive different answers, such as they don't make enough money, they don't like their bosses or co-workers, or they just don't like working. Every organization is different but it boils down to the leadership of the organization.

When I was 14 years old I had a job washing dishes at a local eatery. It was my first "real" job that I got an actual paycheck and a whooping $3.25 per hour. I didn't mind the work because I felt kinda important being the person responsible for making sure the customers had clean dishes to eat from. However, over three dozen years later I reflect on it and remember one lady who I thought rode a broom to work. She would yell at me all the time, boss me around and ride my ass like a Shetland pony. It got to the point where, at 14, I would get stressed out when I saw her car there. When I'd get to work and find out she wasn't going to be there, I knew it would be a good day. When she was there, oh boy, look out, she was yelling. As a immature 14 year old, I was a little scared of her but part of me wanted to flatten her tires some day after work, but I didn't! My point is this, we all remember the bad leaders we worked for. I would not call this lady a leader, but she was my superior, regardless of her title, and she was a meanie. Funny how she made such an impact so many years later.

In reflection of your leadership style and your organization, do you try to fit the square peg into the round hole? Do others within the organization do the same? Do you have instances where this was the case, and it did not work? There is a strong likelihood that you do. If so, it is important to realize what you learned from this. If not, how can you avoid it from happening? The answer is easy, if you have to ask yourself if you are trying to fit the square peg into the round hole, well, then you are.

As an analogy to this, there are some situations where the answer is a clear yes, or a clear no. For some situations there are no "maybes" to be had. Imagine you were on a team assigned to assess promotional candidates or entry level candidates. You have a candidate who may be a viable candidate but there is a "but" clause attached to it. Or, perhaps there is hope the candidate will change or adhere to the culture of the organization. Well, the answer is easy. A zebra does not lose its stripes. Hoping someone will change is a great thought, but the reality is they probably will not. If you are a "maybe" on hiring or promoting someone, please call me. I will promptly tell you no and hang up. Not really, I'd probably talk because I'm a sucker for good conversation, but the outcome should be clear: sometimes there are no maybes, be clear and concise. Again, the square peg is not designed to fit into the round hole, period. If you find yourself doing this, press the reset button and start over. Whittling it down could perhaps make it fit, but was it designed to? No.

As current, future, or up-and-coming leaders, use this approach. Do not try to fit the square peg into the round hole.

Again, let's read on...

FREE BEER TOMORROW

I was driving down the road one day and I passed an establishment that had a sign out front. It read, "Free Beer Tomorrow." As a beer lover, I thought this would be a good opportunity for me to go and grab free suds after work. A good pilsner can top off a stressful day, carry on a joyful day or may just break up the monotony of a busy week. So, the next day I put my drinking shoes on and drove to the bar to capitalize on a free brewski. However, when I got there, the sign still read, "Free Beer Tomorrow." As an educated man, I figured I just had the day wrong and decided to wait and go the following day. But on this next day, I experienced the same thing, the free beer was always tomorrow. Frustrating.

By now you get the gist of things. Now, take this analogy and apply this to your leadership style. Do you offer free beer tomorrow? Do you allow your people to offer free beer tomorrow? A leader cannot afford to over promise and under deliver. If you do, you will soon fit into the free beer tomorrow category. This can impact your leadership potential and therefore must be avoided. It may also keep you from being invited to your retirement party.

I recall a situation where I was a young police officer working in an undercover capacity. I was 22 years old and thought of myself as the new Miami Vice. For you young people this is a great reference to look up to. I was wrong but it felt good all the same. Me and many of my fellow agents from across the state were summoned to a meeting in the capitol city where one of the newly appointed leaders wanted to hear from the rank and file. I thought wow, someone is going to listen to us as we bitch about things. The meeting ensued and lasted a couple hours where the leader took in all that we had to say, took copious notes and then made a few promises to us that things would get better. We would be getting better equipment, better communication, better cars, better everything. As we all left to return to our respective districts, there was a warm feeling that a cultural change was being made and we would be recognized for our contributions. I am sure you can guess where this is going. Fast forward 30 days and the leader was fired. During the 30 days nothing happened, no changes, no forward progress, but a lot of lip service. Again, over promised, under delivered and then he got the ax. While I was a young officer, looking back my best guess is that he had high hopes but those above him shot him down, literally, and showed him the door. He wanted to be a pro-employee leader which is a good quality, but those above him used their iron fists to crush him.

The moral of the story is that bureaucracy can get in the way of progress. Thinking there would be free beer tomorrow is a wonderful thought, but the grand reality is there is never going to be free beer tomorrow, ever. If you find differently, call me as I like free beer.

As we discussed previously, there are tough decisions in leadership. We must be up to the task of taking these head on. Everyone procrastinates, we can agree upon that. However, there are some matters that must be dealt with head-on. Burying your head in the sand like an ostrich will not make the problem go away. Rather, it could make it much worse. Leaders must be methodical, meticulous, and focused, which goes without saying. However, we must be mindful that the free beer tomorrow paradox is real, and easy to promise, but hard to deliver.

How do you get your people to avoid the free beer tomorrow paradox? There is not one boiler plate answer that will be the end-all solution to your problems because it does not exist. However, I do have good news for you: this is solvable. First, one of your duties as a leader is to develop other leaders within your organization. What you will find is that monkey-see, monkey-do. If you cut corners, they will cut corners. If you become a slouch, they will become a slouch. If you are lazy, they will be lazy. Get it?

Leaders must be balls to the walls 100% of the time. While it sounds easy, I guarantee it is not. Leaders are also humans and experience peaks and valleys. Leaders have good and bad days. Leaders have problems outside of work. As you are now asking, how do you get around this? The answer is not all too difficult. When you are at work, be at work. When you are not, then be you. Leave work at work, leave home at home. Easier said than done, but nothing in life comes easy, we must work for it.

My brother worked for an automobile plant for many years and had a successful career up until his retirement, which is great. In leading up to his retirement I told him he needed to find something to do with his life otherwise he'd be taking a dirt nap in a few years. We have seen occasions where an individual devotes the majority of their lives to an organization but after they retire they die. Tragic for sure, undoubtedly, and one cannot blame it on the work entirely. However, it does lead to a valid point which bodes to making sure your people have a life outside of work. Such is not to say you should be their social manager but rather encourage your people to get out and about when they are away from work. Work is work and will be there when you get back. I am not saying you should tell them to stop caring or not give a shit about things. Rather, do something outside of work. Do you have any hobbies or special interests that you do with your time? I use a similar analogy when I instruct young entry level police officers. I tell them they should not live, eat, and breathe policing. When they are off duty, get as far away from it as you can. Again, do not give up caring, but dedicate your mind to other things. Do not let things such as work take up space in your brain rent-free. I encouraged these young officers to fall in love, just not at work. If you have not done so already, find your soul mate, but again, not at work. I am not deterring people from falling in love at work but there have been far too many situations where the ending is not as good as the beginning. Think about that for a moment and, odds are, you have likely come across this type of situation.

Moving back to your leadership style, what kind of life do you have outside of work? Are your "friends" your friends because of your position or because of who you are? Do you spend time away from work hanging out with people from work? Do you have an outer circle of friends who are different from you? Cops hang around cops which is not all too uncommon. However, consider it in a different direction whereas your friends and things you do get you away from your work. An inner circle free of work-related friends is be a good idea. Getting away from your work and talking about other things can enrich your life and reduce stress. While I am certainly not an expert, it is a viable concept.

When I took my first police chief position, I suddenly discovered newly found friends. While I knew them before, I did not hang out with them. If I were to see them, I might have passed on a polite "hello" or other mild greeting. However, I did not go to dinner with them, attend parties together or sporting events. I did attend several of these and when introduced to others it was by my title, not who I am. My first name was not "chief" but rather I am "John" which is what my parents named me. At first, I enjoyed the new attention but then shortly thereafter someone needed a favor. While I am all about helping people and have spent a lifetime doing so, this was not the position that I wanted to be in. I can certainly hold my own and be politically correct, but I did not want to be used for that reason. When there was a seemingly minor favor that did not have any impact, that was easy. However, when the favor put me in a precarious position, I was not about to sacrifice things to accommodate someone. Again, I place emphasis on getting away from your work, enjoy your life, get a hobby, volunteer for a non-profit or do something you are good at to make the world a better place. Your position within the organization needs you, but the true you also needs you.

In the "free beer tomorrow" paradox, we need to be cognizant of those who we surround ourselves with. If you are mentoring up-and-coming leaders, share with them the free beer paradox. Again, we all procrastinate but what about those people who do things without having to be told? What about those who bring solutions when they bring you problems? A leader may be good at barking orders or telling people what to do. But the best leaders really do not need to say much at all because their people know what needs to be done and they get it done. Of course, the leader may need to step in and provide direction here and there, but the best of the best have developed their future leaders so the organization can run on all eight cylinders.

In my mid-level management days, I was fortunate enough to have a leader that allowed me to prosper. My leader was not threatened by me nor stood in my way to advance my career. I made it well known that I wished to advance my career and I am thankful that he recognized that. Not everyone is cut out to be a leader, but my leader saw something in me and gave me a lot of support. Do you do the same for your people? Again, respect is earned, not taken. What degree of respect do you show your people? Do they know they are appreciated?

We will discuss whether leaders are made or born in an upcoming chapter. But for now, let's consider the concept. Regardless of your position on the debate, we can probably all agree that there is a little of both. Some may have inherent qualities because of their upbringing, education or how they strive to be a leader. Others may defy the odds and dedicate themselves to being a leader, educating themselves and rising to the top. As a leader, it is up to you to recognize those up-and-coming leaders within your organization and encourage them. I would not rule out the three-to-five-year employee over the 15–20-year employee. Such is not to say you should ignore either, but we must understand that your job of molding future leaders within your organization is a critical part of your job. Again, here's an example. Take a firearms instructor who is teaching young police cadets how to fire a weapon. The instructor has two students: the first is the cadet who learned to shoot in Uncle Bob's farm with all the other kids, or the second person who has never fired a weapon before. Which will be the better student? Here is the answer: the one who has never fired a weapon before. Why? It's simple, they do not have to correct any bad habits. Now, apply this to your up-and-coming leaders. What are some of their bad habits? Yes, we all have them, but what are you doing about it to fix the bad habit?

I used to chuckle when there would be a promotional opportunity that came up at work because in doing so a bunch of folks would sharpen their pencils, start working harder, doing more and kissing ass. While the latter is not preferred, shouldn't they have been doing this all along? Why did they wait until the promotion was posted to start acting like they wanted to be promoted? Did you see the sign on the way to work that read, "Free Beer Tomorrow?" Apparently not. Consider this, made or born, the leader needs to keep a sharp pencil often. When it gets dull, sharpen it. Don't wait until someone tells you to sharpen your pencil, just do it yourself.

I always like it when a young police officer would ask me how they are doing as they are seeking feedback. It is quite easy to draw the distinction between a kiss ass and someone who is sincere and wants to improve themselves. In one case, the officer wanted to share an arrest that was made, and the role played during it. It was a little more than the run-of-the-mill arrest but all the same the officer was proud of the accomplishment. I gave them a pat on the back and congratulated them on the arrest.

To the contrary, some personnel may talk you up to your face but really all they are doing in crawling into your ass. You need to watch for people like this. I would always say, "You don't need to tell me how good I look because I know how good I look." Kidding, of course. Rather, tell me solutions to problems; tell me how you impacted the organization or helped an individual better themselves. If you are, were, or want to be the leader of the organization, what would you want to hear? It is perfectly fine to share a good experience or how you impacted the organization. In doing so, be humble, appreciative, and understanding. Remember, there is plenty of room at the top but even more room at the bottom.

In any organization there are going to be all different types of people which means the leader must adapt. Are you the kind of leader who is leading by being out and about? Are you one with an open door? Or, do you hide out in your office and avoid people? Do you return all your emails and voice messages? Do you stop and talk to the lowest ranking person in the organization? Do you listen when people brag about their kids or share a favorable experience they may have had? Do you know the names of their kids? Have you asked them how they are doing and mean it? Again, it is easy to become engrossed in things and forget about the people-factor of the organization. But remember, the people of your organization are your critical infrastructure. It does not matter the size of the organization or the type of organization it is, it is about the people of your organization. This is a very strong lesson that we need to remind ourselves of constantly.

As I have said again and again, when other police officers would approach me and mention that they want to be a police chief one day, I commend them. I also give them Johnboy's one size fits all piece of advice that applies to all of them: "Do not forget where you came from." If you did not enjoy being treated poorly, then don't treat people poorly. Did you enjoy being praised, recognized, or just talked to by the leader? If so, then do the same. Do you like kissing ass? Do you let others kiss your ass? Remember, nothing will destroy a great employee faster than watching you the leader tolerate and reward the bad ones. Let that sink in.

So, let's summarize here. If you are driving and you see a sign that reads, "Free Beer Tomorrow" then it is likely not going to be true. If you are a chronic procrastinator, then you subscribe to this paradox. If you keep your promises, deliver, and gain the respect of your people, your odds of success will increase. There is a likelihood that you will be invited to your retirement party. While there are no guarantees in life other than death or taxes, your capital will have risen a bit with the rank and file. The effort is worth it, trust me!

You're Not Invited to Your Retirement Party

L eading up to this chapter we have covered a lot of leadership topics and there are more to come. But this would be a good time to evaluate your leadership style and ask yourself if you will be invited to your retirement party. There are several ways to look at this scenario. You have your leaders, like a bosshole, who will have people show up out of obligation and that leader will relish the fact that people show up. The problem is they are oblivious to the fact that they did so out of obligation. Unbeknownst to them, there will be a "party after the party" and he/she will not be invited to it. Perhaps they will hear about it, but either way, others will be celebrating their departure. Is this you?

As a leader you want to be invited to your retirement party. Yes, it is true that you cannot please everyone nor make everyone happy. In fact, it is likely that you cannot go a week without pissing someone off for something. You will likely be blamed for things which you had no control over nor was it a decision you made. Leaders cannot please everyone, and we know this. However, let's look you delivery. When I travel and lecture for first line supervisors, I share a slide that reads:

- Know your people

- Honor your people

- Respect your people

I share the analogy of my daughter. If I am having a bad day and someone wants to lift me up, all they must do is ask me a question about my daughter and it puts things into a different perspective for me. In seventh grade my daughter told me she wanted to pole vault. I immediately saw emergency room visits, broken bones, and a degree of uncertainty. I was wrong. Fast forward a few years and in high school my daughter was a state champion pole vaulter. She set seven stadium records, broke her high school record by 31 inches and won a boat load of awards. She did so well that she received a five-year scholarship to Marshall University (aka We Are Marshall) where she would go on to set the school record there for both indoor and outdoor track. In her senior year she won the Sun Belt Conference indoor and outdoor track meets with a gold medal. Is it safe to say that I am proud of my daughter, of course it is. My previous leaders saw my pride and used this knowledge to bring be up.

I go on to tell my students that when my daughter was in high school, she said she wanted to study criminal justice. This time I kept my trap shut because clearly I was wrong with the concerns I had with pole vault. Clearly dad was wrong, and she has since graduated with a master's degree and a federal law enforcement job a month after graduation at age 23. I never made it to that level!

Here is the logic I am sharing: How well do you know your people? Do you stop and listen to what they are saying to you? There will

always be the "TMI" employee who tells you way too much information but what they are saying is important to them. I always would
say there is one thing in the world that everyone wants, and it is free,
and that is respect. Apply this principle to your people. Do you know
the names of their children? Do you remember their birthdays or
anniversaries? Do you listen to their story about how their son did in
their hockey match or their daughter in her gymnastics competition?
If you do not, then it's time to start. Being involved, that is what a
good leader does.

I realize that if you have a large organization this may not be possible
where you know everyone on a first name basis. Or, because there
are so many, it would take too much time to get to know everyone.
That makes sense, but consider when opportunity does knock and
you meet an employee whom you do not know. Do you look past
them because you are more important to them? Or, do you approach
them and introduce yourself by your first name, not your title in the
organization. The latter will buy you a lot of stock from your people
and they will share it with others. If you shun them and pretend they
don't exist, they will also share this. In doing so, others will likely add
to the story and by the end of the week you became the gunman on
the grassy knoll. In other words, let the good stuff spread fast and
minimize that which can be negatively said about you. You will still get
blamed for shit you had no control over but don't' add to the negative.
Showing respect for people will go a long way.

The quality leader will know, honor, and respect their people. Perhaps you are a leader who does not. If so, the good news is that this can
be changed immediately. However, be careful not to patronize people
because they will see right through you. This will be counterproduc-
tive, and they may be leery of why suddenly you are taking an interest
in something that you have previously ignored. In this instance, own it

and make it right, make things whole and show that you are interested. It is easier said than done when you have deadlines to meet, budgets to complete, memos to write and emails to address. However, the capital that you will develop from this small task will outweigh the extra time that you must spend.

Speaking of respect, how well to you treat others outside of your organization? Do you talk down to others or do you show genuine respect for them? I would enter the police station to find a prisoner handcuffed to a chair and they clearly did something to get themselves arrested. Some were meek and mild while others were combative. At the first opportunity I would go to them and ask a simple question: are you hungry or thirsty? I could care less what they were there for because it did not really matter. What mattered is where their last meal came from. We all take for granted that there is dinner on the table, but this does not apply to everyone. I did not approach a prisoner in this way to score points, lend sympathy or as some other means to get them to confess, calm down or otherwise conform. I did so because they may be hungry or thirsty and that is something that should be addressed. Some told me some colorful words about having sex with myself, but others proved genuine and asked for something to eat or drink. I did not take offense to any part of it as I knew I was being genuine. Small gestures go a long way...add more!

Take all of this and leverage it toward your leadership style. Are you the leader that others want to follow or be like? Or do others look at you and count the days until your retirement is coming. As I had shared previously, our people are our biggest asset. Our critical infrastructure is our people so we need to recognize this. A leader does not bide by a save ass, suck ass, or kiss ass (heard that before?). Our people do not want the same from you. If you treat them with respect 100% of the time, you will likely get the same back. If you expect them to be the first to delve into the respect jar, you will be left waiting. You do not want people to respect you because they must, you want people to respect you because they want to. A good leader is one who shows respect first with no expectation of a return on this investment.

This transitions into the key piece of advice that I have for all future leaders, same analogy in different words. I have had colleagues tell me they would like to apply for a promotion or perhaps become a police chief. There are many different and moving parts to these positions and strict requirements to those who want to fill these roles. My advice to them has always remained static, simple but impactful. I would render the same reply to everyone regardless of the position they sought, never forget where you came from. Simple as that, do not forget where you came from.

There are some who thrust themselves into leadership positions and they feel like it is a license to treat people like crap. They finally get to boss people around. They finally will get the respect they deserve. Right? Wrong!

A leader needs to be humble, firm but fair, impartial along with a host of other traits. When you are traveling along in your journey as a leader, on a regular basis you should ask yourself if you will be invited to your retirement party. It's a fair question and we need to take a close look at ourselves without an enhanced ego. If you must think about the answer, I'll give you a hint: you won't be invited. If the answer is easy, then perhaps you will. However, be mindful that people can easily change their minds. A simple act of disrespect is enough to do it. Such is not to say you need to be a buddy before a leader because that would not help the organization. But if you follow a firm but fair motto, there is a greater likelihood for success.

There is a likelihood that a week will go by when you do not piss someone off. This is the week you are on vacation and not in the office.

Aside from this, the probability is high that you will piss someone off. The difference here is how it is done. If you do something purposeful-ly, then you are not a good leader. There are going to be some who are a colossal pain in your ass. Here's my advice: get used to them, you will always have them. Do not write them off, do not ostracize them, just work with them. There are some who can never be pleased no matter how much money you give them, no matter how many perks you give them or how much recognition they may get. Consider this, have you ever investigated why this person is so unhappy? Do they have issues outside of work they are bringing to work? Is there a trigger that sets them off? I am not talking about people shooting up the place, but maybe there is something at work that is causing them to be unhappy. The point is this: have you tried to fix things? Yes, it is easy to write someone off and hope they leave. Addition through subtraction in other words. This is going to happen and when it does, ask yourself this, have you tried everything?

If all else fails, perhaps you can consider a one-on-one conversation with this individual, to bury the hatchet. The point being you are making a concerted effort to help this individual. Or, worse yet, what happens when you have a conglomerate that are unhappy with you or the organization. It is not rocket science here, but have you tried to meet with them? Have they listed their grievances to you? I'm not saying you should give up on them or let the tail wag the dog, rather, let's take a seat at the table and try to remedy things.

This leads to compromise which is essentially both parties giving in a little bit to meet a common ground. All too frequently there is a personality conflict or an outlier who is butt hurt and cannot give in. In cases like these, they clearly do not understand the meaning of the word compromise and dig their heels in simply because they can. The leader may have the upper hand but if he/she is refusing to budge then perhaps you are a part of the problem? There is a difference between giving in and compromising. I have seen instances where a boat load of money was blown on principle. I read an article one time that the average loss of revenue to businesses in the United States is around $5 billion dollars from a lack of listening. Somewhere in that huge number rests circumstances where some will cut off their nose to spite their face. The bottom line is it could be costly for the organization simply because one person wants to shove it down someone else's throat. Here's my response: bad idea. Sometimes the greater good needs to be looked at and one's personality and the conflict it is creating for them must be reevaluated. If the leader is willing to mortgage the future of the organization or waste dollars on principle, this leader needs to reconsider.

In terms of being invited to your retirement party, this leader will not be, point blank. The leader who is out and about, available, respects his/her people, blames soft but praises loud, and earns respect versus taking it, then they will be invited to their retirement party. One mistake a leader can make is taking things for granted. As humans we all do this and are guilty of this to some degree. We take for granted our people will show up to work and do their jobs. We take for granted that we will have good health or that our safety is guaranteed. Well, the news is this: we cannot take anything for granted. Easier said than done as usual, but when is the last time you have sat back and realized how you do take things for granted?

Hitting the pause button temporarily, let's switch hats to someone who is going through a tough time. We all have. Say you just lost a loved one, or are experiencing a life change, you are getting a divorce or have been separated from the one you love with all your heart. There are many ways to experience these life challenges and they are difficult, no doubt. Lord knows I have had my share. Despite these times I have always remembered something someone told me a long time ago: "God will never give us anything we cannot handle." I am a believer that all things happen for a reason. Sometimes we know why, other times we are left guessing. It is easy to tell others how to fix their problems and tackle life's challenges. However, how good are we at tackling our own? I have found myself in this position where I was the to-go guy. If a person was having a problem, they would call me, and I would help them or give them advice. I would see others who are facing difficulties and step in to help them. If a person was down, I'd try to bring them up. The problem was that I became good at this for others but was failing this for myself.

The easy answer is to seek out others who may be able to be you and help you with your problems. But what happens when you do not feel comfortable in sharing those problems and you compartmentalize them or internalize them? You are the leader and are not allowed to have problems or experience personal challenges, right? Wrong. You do, and you will. The key will be how you handle these. I will share that internalizing them may be a good temporary fix. Imagine a water balloon and when you start to fill it, it expands and makes room for the water. But what happens when you put too much water into it? It bursts, right? Well, I am not a clinical professional nor expert in human behavior, but I am human and have experienced challenges, death, life changes, and more. I was good at internalizing my problems and showing others that I was this impregnable force, Teflon, strong and able to withstand whatever life threw at me. I was wrong. I was none of this but rather allowed things to get the better of me where it started to impact my quality of life. I was losing my zest, zeal, drive and motivation. I felt like I was on an island by myself with no one to talk to, no one whom I could trust to hear me and no light at the end of the tunnel. From what I have learned, this is not too

uncommon. For me it was new. I had never felt this way. I was always
bursting with confidence and able to withstand life's challenges. But I
wasn't. I discovered my human side that experiences life's challenges.
With more reasons to be happy than sad, I was sad. With many rays
of hope in front of me I did not have any. I could not understand
why this was happening to me because it was something I have never
experienced in my lifetime. I became worried about my own mental
health and whether this life change was going to have an adverse effect
on my future. It is not an easy road to travel, and I wish there was a
one-size-fits-all answer that I could give to you that helped you cope
with your problems. Unfortunately, there is not one. However, on
a favorable note, I am here to tell you that there is an answer. As in
many things in life, you have to go and find it. Nothing in life comes
easy and the road to success has many bumps, ups and downs and an
occasional detour. However, as I noted before, there are no shortcuts
to anyplace worth going. If you are in that rut, seek out help. If you are
down, find a way to lift yourself up. Reach out to others, read a book
(like this one) or write your feelings down as I am doing here. You can
do this, you can find the answers you seek, you can prevail. There are a
lot of negatives in life, and it is easy to fall prey to this. We must avoid
this at all costs which sometimes may include putting ourselves first.
This is not a selfish act as I learned because I was that way. I seldom put
myself first but then discovered it is okay to do that, especially when it
comes to the betterment of yourself. Putting yourself first may help
you climb out of that rut you are in; it may bring back the real you and
help you answer the questions you have been asking yourself.

If people notice a difference in you, then it is quite apparent and
when they speak of it the change has likely been ongoing, not something that just happened today where the red flag is flying outside
your office door. When this happens, it is okay to tell others you are

having personal challenges and you are dealing with them. You may be surprised the response you get. I was. I had ask me if I was alright. I told them I was, and they told me I was lying, which I was. I distinctly remember the conversation, they said to me, "Come on, I know you, I know something is not right with you, please talk to me." I let my guard down and shared my challenges, which was like the first step toward me overcoming them. It was not an easy road, but the journey started then and there.

I realized that I did have a different side to me and that it was okay to accept it, own it and overcome it. It would be nice to flick a switch and things go away and become all hunky dory. We know this does not happen and sometimes problems take time to overcome. However, we cannot let the water balloon continue to fill up and risk letting it burst. Some have done this and it is still recoverable, but likely a little more difficult versus stepping up before it reached this point. Again, easier said than done. We all have cellular telephones. Consider browsing through your contacts and ask yourself who would be willing to listen to you? Or, who can you confide in? The list may be small, but there is a great likelihood that someone in there will. Think about it...

I realized through many experiences that I can be invited to my own retirement party. But to do so, I have to be me. I have to be the person who I am true to, not what someone else may want me to be or how I want others to think of me. I wanted to be liked by others, but not at the sake of having to kiss their ass. I wanted to be liked for who I am, not what I am. This was very helpful for me. While the date has not arrived yet of this writing, I keep hope that I will be invited to my retirement party...

SUCCESS THROUGH FAILURE

If you've never failed, you've never lived.

Life consists of successes and challenges, peaks and valleys, and a whole host of other emotions along the way, some good, some not. Apply all of this to leadership. As a leader you will have ups and downs, good times and bad, wins and losses, but in the end, to be a successful leader, you must have experienced all of these and more. Such is not to say you should seek out failures because unfortunately they will come on their own. Of course, we try to minimize these but there is essentially no way to completely avoid them.

The 16th President of the United States of America Abraham Lincoln who endured many of these emotions. During his lifetime before his presidency, Lincoln lost several elections, lost his job, lost his fiancé who died, and he had a nervous breakdown. He mentioned he had several slips along the way but never fell. He went on to be a highly successful President and fought for equal rights. What would have happened if he gave up?

Here are a few of Abe's quotes that are relative:

"You cannot escape the responsibility of tomorrow by evading it today."

"Most folks are as happy as they make up their minds to be."

"My greatest concern is not whether you have failed, but whether you are content with your failure."

Let's look at Walt Disney. Many of us have visited one of Disney's parks as children or taken our children there. Walt ran into his own challenges, one where he was fired from a newspaper for a lack of imagination and no good ideas. He also had to file for bankruptcy before reaching his ultimate success in the creation of the Walt Disney Company. Can you imagine how things would be without Disney?

Take a look at a few quotes from Walt:

"It's kind of fun doing the impossible."

"All our dreams can come true, if we have the courage to pursue them."

"If you can dream it, you can do it."

Last, how about someone who is arguably the GOAT of basketball, being the greatest of all time, Michael Jordan. When Michael was in the 10th grade, he was cut from the varsity basketball team, then he went home and cried. Fast forward to his professional basketball career where he now holds six National Basketball Association championships and a host of records.

Here are a few of Michael's quotes that may resonate with you:

"The key to success is failure."

"Failure makes me work even harder."

"I've never been afraid to fail."

There are many others but for the purposes of this chapter, lend some thought to these quotes and then apply them to you. It is inevitable that a leader will experience failures. There are many examples of how people have prevailed after a failure. Simply because you have failed does not mean you need to give up. Rather, take this failure, find a positive side to it, and try again. Sometimes we must press the reset button and start over, and sometimes more than once. This could be personally or professionally. We do not set out to fail, that's a given. But some of the things we are involved in may end up in failure. I would always say that a true test of one's character is when they face adversity. Do they hold themselves accountable or blame others? Do they give up or do they try again? How do you handle situations when faced with adversity?

You knew it was coming and yes, here is my example. As a police chief I had a very good track record having worked in law enforcement for over 20 years. During this time, I was impactful and had many successes, along with a few challenges along the way. Ultimately as the police chief I felt I was doing well but began to experience bumps in the road. I was under contract with a severance clause which I chose to execute. I chose to take my toys and go home. There were stressors of the job and difficulties with the administration. It came to the point where I was being questioned about everything I did, despite following in the same footsteps of the chief before me. The writing was on the wall, and I read it loud and clear. There were some who ostracized me, others who wondered what the hell I did to make me leave, and a lot of others whose speculation was that there was a cover-up or something that I was hiding. Unfortunately for them there was no smoking gun, there was no wrongdoing, there was a difference of opinion and philosophy and the last place I want to be is someplace where I am not wanted. It did not come easy and was quite difficult setting aside the profession I love, but eventually it turned out to be one of the best moves I have made.

While I kept my feet in law enforcement, I decided using my talents in higher education was the way to go and I had much success to this end. I began to teach criminal justice courses for undergraduate and graduate students. I authored nearly a dozen courses and was well received by the university. I enjoyed this but part of me felt that my journey was not complete. Then, in 2013, along came a police chief opportunity so I dove in headfirst.

Once I was back in the saddle, I brushed off a little bit of the dust and hit the ground running. Little did I know that it would be harder before it was easier, but with persistence, hard work, and dedication I was able to rise and excel. In fact, I found far more success in this new position than I would have ever had in my former position. While I am not about getting rewards or being recognized for my work, I had the good fortune of both. I was the recipient of federal and state awards for my work in helping families who had missing loved ones. I was recognized for outstanding service by my employer and held several key positions in addition to my chief duties. All the while I kept teaching higher education for two universities.

Does this make me any better than anyone else? Of course not. But it does show how one can face a difficult situation, or perhaps a failure, then turn it into a success. Yes, it clearly does. I would always hear people say to me, "If I can do it, you can do it." That sounds good from the person saying it versus the one hearing it. But the reality is true, if you remember my quote from earlier where my high school football coach said, "Wish in one hand and shit in the other, which one weighs more?" At the time I did not let that quote resonate the first time I heard it, but dozens of years later, this coach proved he was a genius. He knew what he was talking about in life. You can wish for all you want and yes sometimes wishes would come true. But the reality is that most of the time they don't. What comes true is what we put our minds to. What comes true is how hard work and dedication can pay off. Of course, there will be challenges along the way, we all face them.

But ask yourself this question, if you are driving home tomorrow and run into a road closed sign, are you going to stop and wait for them to re-open the road? Or are you going to find a different way home? The answer is obvious, you are going to find another way home. Apply this to any challenge you are facing. Are you going to sit and wait for it to fix itself or are you going to do something about it?

Giving up is very easy, takes little effort and may give temporary satisfaction. But in the long run, giving up is synonymous with regret. Unfortunately, many of us have regrets, I wish it were otherwise. All we can hope for is that we have learned from this regret and saw a silver lining in it. As leaders we need to minimize regret, stay on track, but doing so with the understanding we will encounter failure along the way. How we deal with this failure will eventually define us. As a warning, it is inevitable that it will happen several times, at minimum. Again, these will define us, make us better leaders, and allow us to develop confidence, strength and continue to take our organizations to the next level. While you do this you can also bring the up-and-coming leaders with you. If they are your successor, you will both be glad you did.

There will be times when you get your wings clipped, your lunch handed to you or perhaps a proverbial foot broken off in your ass. You may piss someone off by something you said or did, likely inadvertently, but you did it all the same. Hopefully it was by accident and not intentional, but it happens. A key to success is how you handle it when it is brought to your attention. Do you take ownership of a mistake you made or a decision that may not have been the best? Or do you defend a wrong with a wrong? As I have mentioned, respect is earned, not taken. If you want people to respect you, then you need to take ownership when you make a mistake. Odds are you have worked with or know someone who will go to extremes to defend a mistake even though they know it is wrong. Hopefully these are not folks in leadership positions but if they are perhaps consider buying them a copy of this book and give it to them.

When we look at success through failure, you will not be alone in this arena. Those around you will also encumber failures to various degrees and it will be up to you to help them get through these. Sometimes they may have to figure things out for themselves, but an occasional mistake may lead them to the promised land. Remember, one of your jobs is to develop the leaders underneath you. If you are not subscribing to this philosophy, then perhaps you should rethink things. Leaders do not stand on a plateau by themselves and take credit for all the successes of an organization and blame others when there are failures. Rather, a leader stands on the plateau and reaches his/her hand down to others so they can join. Leaders help them up to the plateau and commend them for reaching it. Leaders do not grease the edges of the plateau so every time they get close they slip and fall off.

Your leadership style may vary from others but let's revert to the dialogue about your retirement party. If you are the one standing on the plateau by yourself, I wouldn't make plans because you are not going to be invited to the party. The amount of respect you will gain from helping other leaders prosper will pay dividends. As leaders we have to keep in mind that the end always comes no matter what. There will be a day when you are no longer the leader of the organization and someone else will take over. If you are invested in the organization and want to see it succeed, then you need to take time to develop the up-and-coming leaders from within. You cannot give up on them despite some of the pitfalls that exist. An easy way to look at this is to revisit the road that you traveled to become a leader. Odds are the road was bumpy and there were peaks and valleys. However, you prevailed and likely had some help along the way. If you are an aspiring leader, don't be afraid to reach out your hand to others if you want to maximize your leadership potential. If you have any respect for the organization you will want to see them carry the torch after you leave and prosper, not fail. If you are a leader who wishes for the organization to falter, it is time to rethink why you are in this position

There are some leaders who like to play with their own toys and keep them all to themselves. This may bode well with others outside of the organization as they will purport themselves as being highly successful, but the reality is they will let no one into their ring nor help develop other leaders. The outsiders may cast a favorable light onto this leader and put them on a pedestal. The degree of success may last for a bit but eventually this leader will need some help or run into challenges that may warrant others coming to their rescue. We can only hope that the others will do so but if they don't, some may not blame them.

When you read books like this and others, those writing it may make leadership sound easy. Just like the "If I can do it, you can do it" statements which also make it sound easy. But, if we sit around and relish failure, we cannot succeed. Let's face it, nothing in life comes easy. In case you don't remember, there are no shortcuts to any place worth going. The light at the end of the tunnel is waiting for you to dig your way there. Your defining moment is not isolated to one instance, it's a lifetime of experience that leads you to many defining moments.

THE COOL-AID

Oh yea! As kids there was nothing more refreshing than an ice-cold glass of Kool Aid. I remember the commercials where the Kool Aid Man would come jumping out with the slogan "Oh yea!" It is a delicious drink with many fine flavors, but it is not the kind of drink I am referring to when it comes to leadership. Rather, this is called the "cool-aid."

As I refer to this, you have probably heard some sort of jargon about drinking the cool-aid in various forms or degrees. It is almost like a cult following. In simple terms, they are inferring that someone is either sucking up to the administration or in some ways being a suck ass, save ass, or kiss ass. They are believing in the unbelievable, or perhaps have their heads so far up the leader's ass that they cannot see clearly. Or, they have lost sight of their upbringing...you know, where you treat others as you want to be treated.

As the leader of any organization there is a likelihood that others will talk about you behind your back. Don't worry, this is common-place. If you have the mindset that those people should take a number and step in line, you may be alright. However, we must be very careful because this "talk" behind your back could have some logic to it. Are you brewing up cool-aid every morning when you arrive? Do you have others who will believe you that it is snowing in Florida in July? Do you have people who laugh at your dumbass jokes? Be mindful, they are drinking your cool-aid. Do you have moles that come running to you and spill the beans on that which the rank and file is saying about you? Perhaps so, but then again, is that someone embellishing along the way or are they speaking the truth? In either case, we cannot completely turn a blind eye to it.

Leadership includes having the talent of seeing things that are invisible. The water cooler talk may be full of invective or venom that is being spewed by those people whose misery cannot be fixed. For example, a person like this would win the lottery then bitch because they had to split it with another winner. If that's you, please reach out to me as I'll be more than happy to take half of the money, that way you don't have to worry about it.

In real terms, we can all agree that some folks will not be happy, regardless of what we do or what is given to them. However, what about those who may have some legitimacy to their complaints? To see things invisible the leader must be open minded to listen to what is being said behind his/her back. It is a difficult problem because you cannot fix what you do not know is broken. As you are reading this you are probably asking yourself "how do I address this problem?" The answer is not all too difficult. Are you the type of leader who is approachable? Do your personnel feel comfortable coming and speaking to you? Or is there a mechanism in place that allows others to share their thoughts, issues, or complaints freely without rear of repercussion? If they do not have such a means, you must create one. I say this because sometimes as leaders we must share difficult truths. On the same token, we must also hear difficult truths, listen to them and react. This may include truths about us and how others see us. Receiving criticism is never easy but it is also synonymous with growth and development. We live in a world where you cannot go a day without reading the news where someone is apologizing for something they said or did because it offended someone. We cannot be offended when we receive hard truths about ourselves or the organization we are tasked with leading. Again, as a leader, you cannot fix what you do not know is broken. Sometimes people need to tell you what is wrong, and you have to adapt to it. This is not a bad thing so be sure to stay open-minded. By doing so you will garner respect from others, simply because you are listening to them, you are hearing them, and you are willing to adapt versus digging in your heels.

As we look at the cool-aid, we must also look at how we brew it ourselves. Do you pop into work each morning and brew up a fresh pot of cool-aid? Are others kissing your ass and when you stop walking, they run into you? A good leader needs to be able to see through this, be independent and avoid brewing this drink? For those of you out there whose boss brews the cool-aid, you are probably asking yourself how you handle this. The answer is easy, you don't handle it. Rather, you get your ass up and moving, speak up and let them know. Right, it is easy to walk into the office of your boss, sit down and tell him/her that they are pissing people off or acting in a way that will not get them invited to their retirement party.

If you care about the organization and are an up-and-coming leader, it is time to step up. Perhaps do not march into the boss' office and start pushing your weight around. Instead, find that mechanism that allows you to do so. For example, if there is something you want, it is likely not best to ask this on a Monday morning. After a nice and relaxing weekend, we are back to the office and need to brush off all the dust we accumulated over the weekend. I worked for a boss like this once and I quickly learned to wait until he was in a good mood to ask him something. It worked too because reading him like a book helped and I was able to get things done through him during those times unlike when he would come in, walk into his office, and shut the door. Set DEFCON 4 when this happens, sometimes higher.

As a police chief my officers would joke about the red, yellow, and green flags that are outside of my door. Like those that you see outside the patient rooms in a doctor's office, these imaginary flags would dictate when officers could (or would) approach me about something. The flags did not exist but moreover important was how they recognized when a good time was to approach me. As a leader we strive to do our best to be that person who never has a bad day, never lets things bother them and tackle the world every day.

Yes, there are some people who ignore all the signs and walk into a room full of boxing gloves dressed as a punching bag. People like this do not see things invisible, have a track record of TMI (too much information), ignoring the obvious not knowing when to shut up, and are just inherently annoying. However, as leaders we must look beyond this and recognize the value of every employee, not just a certain few. One way to do this is through simple communication and effective listening. All too often we become engrossed in the pile of work that is waiting for us, the several dozen new emails that popped up in the last hour or the line of people waiting to speak to you. We must stop what we are doing, look to the individual and hear them out. Some people just want to be heard. I have seen this many times and if you do not listen to them, you may miss something. If you are the type of leader who writes off certain people for certain reasons, you must reconsider. All your people have differing degrees of value and this needs to be considered. We need to avoid the good ole boys club and ensure this does not become institutional or a norm because it can be difficult to overcome. Remember, you hold the keys to the organization and set the tone. If you allow it to happen, it will.

Another key to the cool-aid saga is whether it is brewed when you are not there. In leadership, it is not what happens when you are there, it is what happens when you are not there. As John Maxwell said, "The leader knows the way, shows the way, and goes the way." We cannot subscribe to the analogy, "when the cat is away the mice will play." It is understood that some may act a little differently when you are not around than how they act when you are there. However, are they getting the job done? Are they behaving as you expect them to or are they slouching? Someone must be in charge when you are not there. Or, depending on the depth of your organization there could be many others in charge when you are not there. All the same, are they carrying out the mission? You also want to make sure they are not brewing their own flavor of cool-aid. Yes, we entrust others to take charge and do the right thing when no one is looking. However, if the other leaders within the organization are creating a brand of cool-aid, look out because this will be impactful on the organization. Such is not to say others cannot form their own style of leadership different from yours because this is a good thing. What I am referring to is the cool-aid where they are iron fisting their way to having others follow them or adhere to their rules. Or, worse yet, they are creating an environment in the workplace that is isolating others or causing division.

Here is an example: as the leader of an organization, you are going to have to make decisions. Some will be more critical than others, some will be more impactful than others. There is a difference between personal and personnel. If you are making these for the former, you need to reconsider. A key difference is how your leadership team handles this. Or, if you are a part of the leadership team, how do you handle it? If you disagree with your leader's decision then you need to speak up, voice your concerns and be heard. If you are the leader, then you need to listen to those who do this. Ultimately, when everyone leaves the room, there needs to be a clear understanding of the decision.

The leadership team cannot go behind the back of the leader and bad mouth the decision. The leadership team needs to be supportive of the decision. Yes, I know, easier said than done. However, if you have voiced your concerns and attempted to iron them out, at least you have demonstrated you took them into account. If you are the leader and listened to what your team has to say but did not change your position, then so be it. A key to success here would be in the delivery. This could be referred to as a "buy-in" but really should be a "sell-in" by the leader. If the leader has empathy, understanding and the ability to relate to people, the delivery of the decision could go smoothly. I am a firm believer that when you treat people fairly, respect them and are honest with them, they will do the same for you. While they may not agree with your decision, at least they will respect it.

If the leader does not deliver the decision in a respectful manner, he/she can run the risk of others following under protest bad mouthing the decision. You would rather have them support the decision publicly and work to help others to adhere to it? This is not putting the square peg in the round hole and should not be confused as such. It should be more focused on how the decision was reached, how it was delivered and its impact on the organization. The leadership team needs to support its leader and only behind closed doors can speak up, be heard, and make sure they understand. Again, this is not easy, but no one ever said being a leader was, right?

In terms of the cool-aid, if the leadership team does not agree with the decision but publicly supports it, do not confuse this with drinking the cool-aid. If parts of the team did not speak up, then perhaps they took a couple gulps or sips of the cool-aid. As leaders within an organization, whether you're the head cheese or a part of the leadership team, you must have moral courage. In other words, moral courage means guts. Such is not to say that you should throw a fit if you don't get your way or continue to bitch piss and moan until you do, but rather use your guts and speak up. Decisions are not always easy, especially when you are on the receiving end of a decision you do not agree with. There are many ways to look at this and one key aspect to consider is it is not life threatening. So take a calm look at it, analyze it and be open minded to it. As I mentioned earlier, as a leader it is perfectly fine to reverse your decision. The analogy I used of digging in your heals makes good sense. It is not a sign of weakness if you change your mind. It is something that is likely to gain you respect because your decision may not have been the best and you took input from others and made the situation right.

Looking at what we gleaned from the cool-aid. It's not Kool Aid, but cool in a sense that you do not want to brew it, drink it nor create your own flavor of cool-aid. Your leadership style is yours and you should be free to exercise it. In doing so, you need to avoid brewing and sharing the cool-aid. Keep the organization moving forward, avoid the good ole boys club and always remain open-minded.

More to come...

GENERATION WTF

I would be remiss if I did not include this chapter in the book. It is about the next generation, of course depending on when you read this. There were the Baby Boomers, The Gen X, The Millennials, Gen Z and now Gen Alpha. I call it the generation WTF and you can break that down and define it however you like.

As leaders there will be a time when we are dealing with the next generation, regardless of where you fall in line with the others. I wish for a magic key that will minimize or eliminate all the challenges that go along with generational differences, but I am afraid one does not exist. In consideration of dealing with this generation, I tried to put my feet into the shoes of leaders I had and tried to imagine how they dealt with me and my generation. I can say that my generation did not get butt hurt very easily, did not get offended all too easily and we appreciated a 40-hour a week job with no sense of entitlement. I am confident there were other things we possessed that annoyed the hell out of the leadership, but these were not the culprits. The question looms, how in the hell did we survive or how the hell are we going to survive?

As of the writing of this book, the next generation facing us has a sense of entitlement, does not want to work, and wants to be paid bank. There should be no ladder to climb to success, it should be handed to them on day one. You should be honored to have them grace your presence and give them anything they want to make them happy. We can all agree it is not possible.

Like a chameleon, leaders must adapt to their surroundings and there is no way around this. As has been said before, this is much easier said than done. Whatever the next generation holds, we are going to have to somehow adapt to it. It would be a noble attempt to have them adapt to us, but the reality is this will not happen. So, you are probably asking yourself how we do this? The answer is not all too difficult and is probably right in front of you. If there were one simple answer that would be nice, but alas, there is not. However, there are several that you may find helpful.

As has been said throughout this book, respect is earned, not taken. Respect is a two-way street and should start from the top. By showing the new generation some respect, this is a good start. If you expect them to respect you, consider taking the first step. Remember, you are the experienced one who is now their leader, and they will look up to you. However, they will only look up to you if you treat them with respect. Hazing the new generation or trying to mold them into something they are not will lead to resentment which will lead them to walking out the door and you could lose an asset. Make no mistake, the tail does not wag the dog and as the leader you do not need to be a save ass, kiss ass or suck ass, nor do they.

If you start with an iron fist and demand respect, good luck. It may work on some, but it will not work on all. It will cause resentment and will spread like wildfire and like all fires, they burn fast in an upward fashion. I am not suggesting you become the BFF of the new generation or somehow sing kumbaya with them. You should, at minimum, show your appreciation for them which can be done respectfully while laying the groundwork of expectations. Communication goes a long way and will add to levels of respect earned.

I recall hiring a young police officer who was fresh out of the police academy. This individual was just over age 21 and the job was his first real one. He seemed to enjoy police work and did a decent job. However, about four months into it he asked me when he would get weekends and holidays off. At first, I thought I was on candid camera and was waiting for the host to jump out from behind a closed door and have a laugh on me. I suddenly realized he was being serious. Having worked a boat load of nights, weekends, and holidays for over 15 years, I could never have imagined going to my boss and asking him that question. But he was serious and felt that he should be granted these because he had been here for several months. Smartly I took the question in stride as I wanted to put off the question. What I really wanted to do was grab a rubber hose and smack him upside the head (really, not really). If you want banker's hours, then you should have been a banker. Cops work nights, weekends, and holidays, period. Crime does not stop during these times. It took me a while to process this question because he was so serious about it and really wanted it granted to him. He felt the department was obligated to accommodate him and make him happy.

On a similar note, another young police officer approached me and wanted more time off work, like vacation and personal time. I think the officer felt as though I had a magic wand in my office which could fill his personal time off bank full of endless time to take off work whenever they felt like it. Again, the officer was serious. Once again, I could not imagine asking this of my boss when I was a young police officer but here we go again, yet another unusual request that I did not expect to ever receive.

I took time to process this as well and pondered many thoughts. I was asking myself if this was the next generation of cops and what would they want next. Over the years I have learned that there are certain things that make people happy and sometimes these can be little things, like showing them respect. But I have also learned that sometimes there isn't anything that will be the end-of-all solution to make people happy. For example, a person gets a nice raise and for a period they are happy, or moreover content. Unfortunately, it will not last all too long. There will soon be a replacement for what they are unhappy about which will leave you digging for answers. When you do find an answer, you press the repeat button. It may make them happy but again this will be temporary. Your treasure chest of warm fuzzies is empty and to them it will now feel like cold pricklies. Let's face it, they are not happy nor may ever be.

When this point is reached, they may consider leaving or, worse yet, staying and being eternally disgruntled. In the world of leadership, we have what is commonly referred to as the 80/20 rule. It means that 80% of your problems are caused by 20% of your people. This means you will spend an exorbitant amount of time dealing with the twenty percenters. Any organization, large or small, it is still a lot of people and a lot of problems.

I am not suggesting you clean house and show people to the door. But, in some cases, there is addition through subtraction, and it is likely you have seen this at some point in your life. I am suggesting that we try to find a happy medium where you can please your people but not at the expense of the organization. I would tell others that salvation lies within and by all accounts they have something else going on in their lives or they are just simply a glass half-empty person who sees the negative before they see the positive. People like this exist and as leaders it is up to us to try to change their mindset and look at the glass as being half-full. In doing so, you could be doing them a great service for their entire life. Advice is only as good as what is followed.

This leads us to situations when we encounter the askhole. The person who falls into the category of an askhole is one who asks a lot of questions or asks for advice, then does not follow it or does the opposite of what you tell them. The sad news is there is a lot of this that goes on with the newer generations. It does not make them bad people; it is just their generation. If you are a parent, odds are you tried like hell to have your children avoid some of the issues or problems you had growing up. But sometimes we all must learn the hard way. Apply this same principle to your people. You try to give them notable advice, lead them to the promised land yet they choose to take a shortcut which will not work.

In a perfect world everyone would listen effectively to their bosses or elders and have a problem free life. Of course, we all know that is impossible. However, consider an approach where you can be impactful in delivering your advice to the next generation in a way it sticks. As I mentioned, we must be the chameleon and adapt. Such is not to say you give in and let them boss you around, or cater to their every whim, but rather understand their wants and needs and try to find a common ground. The key will be to understand their common ground. It is likely to be vastly different than the common ground in which you were raised in.

So, when you look at the next generation and say "WTF" you are not going to be too far off kilter and perhaps you are not wrong. But you also have to remind yourself that when they are looking at you, are they also saying "WTF?" The odds are they will be thinking this, but then again, in math, isn't two negatives a positive? Yes, it is. Use this to your advantage and grasp ahold of the concept of being different with the understanding there is common ground, room for compromise and adaptation. Giving up on the generation will not work because they are the future leaders. I get it, this may be a scary thought. But remember, the same principle was applied to you when you were a young leader and look at where you are at.

I recall a young officer coming to work and the jeans they were wearing were essentially ripped to shreds. I would never comment on how someone is dressed as this is a personal choice and to each their own. However, another officer commented on the pants to which the officer noted how expensive they were. I was thinking to myself, who the hell would pay a lot of money for these jeans. I guess I already knew the answer to that question. When I was asked for my opinion on them, I suggested they go to Goodwill, buy a pair of jeans, and bring them to my house, and I would run them over with my lawn mower and they'd look the same. They didn't think it was all too funny, but I did. I guess it is a sign of the times where in my day a rip in your jeans was not cool but apparently now it is, very much so. It's hard to say what the future will hold so strap yourself in as it is coming right at you.

The bottom line, generation WTF is here to stay and there is more to come. You cannot beat the generation and it will be fruitless to try. However, the good news is there is light at the end of the tunnel for everyone, you just need to work your way there, in peace and harmony.

BUTT HURT

The perfect place for this chapter is immediately following Generation WTF. You see, as a follow-up to that generation and that we must deal with now, is the degree of people being butt hurt. When I first heard the phrase butt hurt, I was a bit baffled before I placed it into perspective. It is quite fitting in many situations but mostly with that which leaders must deal with. Such is not to say leaders cannot be butt hurt because they are just as vulnerable as anyone else. However, today, we cannot read a news application, website or even watch the news without someone who was offended by something or someone.

Rewind the clock many years ago and imagine if I were to tell you someone would buy a hot cup of coffee at McDonalds, spill it on themselves, get burnt, sue McDonalds and win $1M. I would have been laughed out of the room, mocked, and ridiculed. Today, well this is quite common. I remember the fall of 1988 when I attended the basic police academy when one of the instructors told us this: anyone can sue anyone anytime for anything. Not too surprising it was engrained in my mind all these years later, but it still holds true, but exponentially.

The same can be about people who are easily offended. Make no mistake, there are some dipshits out there who say things that are way out of line. There is not a shortage of them. However, in the workplace, leaders must be super careful, to say the least. Such is not to say they should hole up in their office and hide, because that will not work. Rather, be mindful of what you say. There are a number of reasons, other than the obvious. First, what you say as a leader can be looked at as binding, precedent setting, or etched in stone. If you say it, you better mean it. You may think others do not listen to you, but I am here to tell you they do. It may be selective at times but nonetheless they still hear you. Jokes are funny and make people laugh, but jokes can generally offend someone, and it is not all too difficult to do so.

As you are reading this you are probably asking yourself how to handle those who easily get butt hurt, offended, or just easily bothered. You have heard the slippery slope clause, and this is one of them. There is not a shortage of people in this category but there are also others who are rabblerousers who just want to stir the pot. They want to incite angst, get people pissed, then blame someone else for their transgressions. They want to bitch, piss, and moan when things don't go their way or the way of others, although it may not impact them by any means.

While we do have to be careful in what we say, how we say it, and the way it is delivered, we cannot spend the rest of our careers walking on eggshells. The easiest way to approach these situations is to be the chameleon. As leaders we need to adapt to our people, they do not need to adapt to us. It does not mean that you should tell dirty jokes to some and not others as this would be inappropriate regardless. Rather, keep things on the up and up, get to know your people and find common ground. As stated repeatedly throughout this book, respect is earned, not taken. You will be surprised how much respect you get when you show it first.

Leaders tend to have a bullseye painted on them at times. You become an easy target for people who like to bitch, piss, and moan, and sometimes (or often) it's about you. There is an important takeaway here which is to stop and think if there's any validity to what they are saying. As we discussed, some people are just not happy regardless of what you do for them, how much they are paid, or any provisions you do to make their lives easier or better. However, let's look at those who normally wouldn't say shit if they had a mouthful. Is there something you are doing that is offending someone, upsetting them, or otherwise being a Richard (or Karen)? Sometimes we need to reflect on ourselves and while we may feel strongly about a situation, does that mean we are right? Or reflection in terms of taking an honest and realistic look at our inner selves and what we see. While many leaders are their own worst critics, some are their best cheerleaders. Herein, there should be a balance of being modest and confident, but also humble and appreciative. The latter of being appreciative is for the opportunity to lead but for others who want to follow you. I will put the emphasis on "want" because to the contrary "have" or "must" which is not as welcoming.

An experience came to mind with a leader who started off on the wrong foot. Rather than pressing the reset button and starting again, this leader was one with a shovel who just kept digging and digging until they found themselves in a no-win situation. They did not see it as such and yet continued to dig as far as they could go. As a leader, when you look at everyone as a threat to you, there is something wrong. Everyone should be given the chance to be viewed as an opportunity and not a threat. Some will take the low road and will be a threat, but this is a very small minority of people. These individuals will be so obvious that it will not take a rocket scientist to reveal. It will be so evident to you that these individuals will not be getting on the bus with you. In that case, shut the door and get the bus moving. Or, as a related analogy, these individuals will be an anchor, a pimple on the ass of progress, or simply the 80% of the 80/20 rule.

As this leader started off on the bad foot, not only did they view everyone as a threat, but they also viewed everyone as beneath them, an underling if you will. Employees were subordinate to them; pissants, or just bottom feeders. If you refer to yourself as "The Boss" and unless you are Bruce Springsteen, you need to reevaluate yourself. In terms of being boss, this depicts someone who tells others what to do. They are on a plateau by themselves and know everything which is far more than their subordinates will ever know in this lifetime or any other, or so they believe. The boss leader is never wrong, always right, and will never hold themselves accountable. Rather, even when they are wrong, it is someone else's fault. Remember, they are the boss, right? Wrong.

If you are like this, please self-reflect. There is no way possible that you are always right and everyone else is always wrong. There is no way that everyone is against you like some sort of coup like you are being overthrown of your crown. It does not happen this way and maybe it's you. There is no harm in admitting you are/were wrong about something or many things. My advice is to find a champion who has moral courage (i.e. guts, balls, cajónes, etc.) who will be open and honest with you. For leaders it can be difficult to hear when we do things wrong when we think we are doing right. Kudos to those who will tell us because they are your champion. It may not feel like it or seem like it, but they are doing you a favor. It may be hard for them to say and harder for you to hear, but in the end, they are helping you despite how it may feel. When you do hear this, if you dig in your heels otherwise and continue to reflect upon the negative, then a champion will do you no good. Rather, it's you; just know, it is never too late to turn things around. The time is always right to do the right thing. This could include admitting you erred and are going to make it right.

I worked for a leader like this. One who was always right, never wrong. One who saw everyone as a threat despite others trying to work together with them. The individual also referred to themselves as the boss and reminded others often that's who they were. Leadership is about teamwork, but this individual was the spitting image of a micromanager, a narcissistic person, and one who took on every position they could despite having fully qualified others who could perform at peak levels and lead the organization to the next level. The leader put individuals into quasi-supervisory roles because they knew they would not disagree with them but rather do exactly what they say whether right or wrong. When this leader says something, others are expected to agree. If you did not always agree, then you were deemed hard to work with, or, worse yet, a bigger threat to this individual. The challenge became a bigger one as time progressed because the individual created a bigger isolation from others and just looked down upon them like they were meaningless and could not hold a candle to their leadership.

Unfortunately, as you could likely predict, it did not end well. The leader was cut off at the knees and given a large shit sandwich in the form of walking papers. Rather than walking out the door quietly and to maintain what little dignity was left, Captain Vindictive came rolling in. The leader had to do everything they could to leave the place in a mess, create even more controversy, and further isolate the organization as a whole. When the end came, it was good riddance. There was a party for this departure, but this person was not invited.

It did not need to be this way as others had tried to work together but it was just not in the cards. In looking back, I wish this individual would have been more open minded. I wish they would have welcomed their leadership team to take the organization to the next level. I wish there was not a "my way or the highway" attitude of iron fist leading. At remote times I felt sorry for this individual because as a person there were friendly qualities, but as a leader, there were very few good qualities. As you will read in a future chapter, we will discuss whether leaders are made or born. Herein, this individual is the exception and not the rule. Their role as a leader leaves a lot to question and is one where the sense of entitlement as a leader got the better of them. Perhaps there are/were some leadership qualities within them, they failed to recognize this, and their tenure was a colossal failure on all ends.

As you are reading this some questions may linger. What is a take-away from this? Are you just badmouthing someone who pissed you off or did not give way to real or perceived threats? The answer is no. When one thinks it's the world against them, it's them. I wished for a better working environment and put forth my best effort and even asked repeatedly to press the reset button in hopes of things changing. It didn't. So, for me the key takeaway to share is this: as a leader, please be open minded, let others help you and work with you, do not view everyone as a threat until proven otherwise. Let your leadership team shine and they will make you shine. I once read something that resonated with leadership and it went like this: seek out others who are better than you, different than you, and braver than you. Bring this to your leadership table.

Looking back, when it comes to being butt hurt, many of us fall prey to this. In applying this to a failed leader, we have to persevere and overcome failure. It may mean pressing the reset button, starting over, or simply just trying again to be that leader your organization needs. As leaders, we have to occasionally be dealt a piece of humble pie and step back a few paces. None of this makes you a bad leader; it makes you human. You can still be a good leader when setbacks happen because they will make you a better. As the analogy goes, what does not kill you makes you stronger. Setbacks will happen, frustrations will happen, people will annoy the heck out of you, but in the end, always remember the good in people, the good in yourself, and the greater good of leadership.

GOING FORWARD IN REVERSE

O ver the preceding nine chapters we have discussed many different facets of leadership. We will slightly change gears here and take things in a bit of a different direction. The analogy of the square peg/round hole was designed to elevate your thinking as it relates to your overall performance as a leader. Moving forward, let's look at the decision-making process you have as a leader.

Leaders make dozens of decisions every day, without question. Some are simple, everyday decisions while others could be impactful on the organization or the people who work in it. As I have said previously, the critical infrastructure of any organization is its people, and they must be valued. However, we must be careful when making certain decisions. I then remarked the difference between personal and personnel and we can apply that case here. We also need to understand the difference between thinking with the brain and thinking with the heart. I will not take sides on whether one or the other should be used because there are viable arguments in favor of both.

Leaders must be forward thinkers. They need to be able to look into the crystal ball and forecast the future. A part of forward thinking is to study the past and use this as a baseline for predicting the future, hence the title of this chapter, going forward in reverse. Some may read this from a glass half full lens which is not all too difficult to do. However, my thinking is from the lens of a glass half full.

There are times when organizations may benefit from addition through subtraction when a disgruntled employee leaves or some other fashion. Herein, we sometimes need to look in the rearview mirror and see what it is telling us. We try to make calculated decisions and polish things to perfection on a regular basis, which goes without saying. What about decisions that were made in the past that did not bode well? Is there something to learn from that? Well of course, there is.

One of the many things I have learned is about the old adage that goes like this: we cannot change this; we've always done it that way. Have you heard of that one before? The problem is that organizations may stick to a decision which may have fit the mold when it was made, but has the organization evolved through time? Decisions must be fluid and it is perfectly acceptable to change them. Digging in your heels and refusing to change a decision will not be the best approach. As I have noted earlier, changing your mind is not a weakness but rather a strength. When I became a police chief I came in from the outside and had to learn the organization from top to bottom. I recall learning many of the decisions that were made before me and when I would ask why, the response was the same, "...because we've always done it that way." Simply because you have does not mean that it was right. We cannot stick with things because they have always been done that way. You must challenge the status quo. Such is not to say you should turn the organization upside down but just be open-minded to making changes.

This transitions us into the role of a change agent. While definitions may vary, leaders should have a clear understanding that change is inevitable and resisting will only keep the organization from moving forward. Such is not to say you must overturn everything, flop it upside down and start all over, as this is not the case. Rather, there is always room for improvement and to think otherwise could also be impactful. As a change agent, leaders will need to get buy-in from their employees. As you know, this is much easier said than done but it is not an impossible task either. Keeping in mind who is your critical infrastructure, for they will be your delivery of the change. My example of this was during the height of the pandemic when vaccinations were becoming available, and organizations were pondering the necessity of these. Our leaders decided to implement a mandatory vaccination policy. Despite opinions, it was deemed lawful at the time and those who refused were subject to disciplinary action up to and including termination of employment. The action is clearly adverse and subjected some to be terminated. There were exemptions to the policy but that is not the focus nor is the legality of the policy.

The issue at hand was the delivery of the policy. There was a strong belief by the creator of the policy, and this belief was cast upon others in a not so nice manner. In short order, it was shoved down our throats. Because I was a department head and spoke against it, I was ostracized to some degree because I would not agree with the policy. My logic was that the vaccination was new, and I hoped to see other major organizations take to it, first like the Cleveland Clinic, University Hospitals or Metro Hospital, all major health care providers in the greater Cleveland area.

Aside from being ostracized over my position, I had no choice but to follow the policy because it was legal and binding. But when I was asked for my opinion, I gave it. If I were to have been asked if I was going to follow the policy, the answer would have been a yes. Many of the staff had already received their vaccinations and because of this they were not impacted by the policy, me included. However, many were mad or upset at the way the policy was delivered. I was put into a precarious position because I did not support the policy but had to enforce it. This brings up two schools of thought. First, as a leader, if you disagree with something, it should be perfectly acceptable to speak your position without fear of reprisal. The same should apply to your people. They too should be free to speak their position without that fear of reprisal. Is that your position?

The second school of thought is how a leader will enforce a policy that they disagree with. The answer is not all that hard. After you have spoken up and made your feelings known, if the decision still stands then you have to enforce it. However, the leader should not go to his/her subordinate personnel and tell he/she disagree and is obeying under protest. This would be very easy to say, and it would take the heat off you. However, what do you think the subordinate people are going to think and act? They probably will not think too highly of those above them and may also feel there is a lack of support or respect. The presence of this will be harmful to the organization and I can attest to this. We had employees who left for other jobs over the policy. It was not the policy because those who left had been vaccinated, but rather they were pissed about the way it was delivered to them. They felt as though they did not matter, their opinions or beliefs did not matter, and that this decision was being shoved down their throats.

Again, we must not lose sight of the spirit of the conversation. This is not about whether an employer can mandate a vaccination because that is for a different book. Rather, our focus should be on the delivery of the policy. If the powers that be would have sat down with department heads and had an open conversation absent of finger pointing and elevated dialogue, it is probable that the outcome would have been better received. Sitting down and telling the employees how much they are valued, which includes their health and welfare. To share the statistical data and perhaps refer employees to their physicians for a determination as to whether they should receive the vaccination. Or seek input from everyone as to their position, weigh the pros and cons and then use that as a consensus to form a decision.

The problem is that none of this happened. Rather, one person's firm beliefs were cast upon others and shoved down their throats. The policy applies to all employees, but it did not apply to the elected officials because technically they were not employees, and the provisions could not require them. Regardless of the argument, consider the message that was being sent. The elected officials were choosing a policy to enact upon its employees, but it did not apply to them. In other words, what is good for the goose was not good for the gander. The pushback from the employees was detrimental to morale, people were upset, angry and there were a lot of emotions. Again, consider the big picture: most of the people were vaccinated so the policy did not impact them but they were still pissed. In sum, there was less than 10% of the employees who were not but the remaining 90% remained upset, rightfully so.

The key takeaway here rests with the decision making by superiors, but also the way it is delivered. Agreeing or disagreeing does not make any difference. Leaders should understand the decisions may not always be well received by their employees. Taking a hardline stance or an iron fist approach is only going to get you resistance and the story I shared is a perfect example of it. The reality of the matter is that the policy would have been better received if better delivered.

Speaking of delivery, as a leader there will be times when you may need to deliver discipline or other dialogue that may not have the best of content. While there is no easy way to deliver a disciplinary message, when an employee breaks policy or does something to get them in trouble. My advice is simple, unless you are terminating the employee for adverse misconduct, try to find the silver lining in the employee, even if it is ever so slight. The purpose of disciplinary action is twofold: one on the punitive side for misconduct of varying degrees. The other is to correct behavior and to get the employee to conform. It is not rocket science but the key is how it is delivered. If you have ever been on the receiving end of dialogue like this, how did it bode with you? Did you have resent in the manner it was delivered? Or, did you respect the delivery and accept it responsibly? Whatever the outcome, you should consider this when you are in that position. It is not easy but if you are one who enjoys these things you need to take a step back.

I think it is safe to say that no one wants to be yelled at, as it does not serve any good purpose. Rather, consider your words as they will speak louder than the tone of your voice. In doing so, you must clearly tell the employee what they did wrong, but you are also giving them an opportunity to correct their behavior. My advice here is simple, try to end the conversation on a favorable note. For example, tell the employee they are valued members of the team, and you want them on board. Or consider trying to build up their confidence by emphasizing their worth. Be careful not to try and blow smoke up their ass because this will not fly, and you will be patronizing them. The words must be true and from the heart. People are people, we make mistakes, we screw up, we are imperfect. But many of us are good people with good hearts and this cannot be forgotten. Remember, for maybe the 100th time, people are the critical infrastructure of the organization. We cannot forget this.

So, in looking at this through the lens of moving forward in reverse, we should keep our eyes on both. We value our people, that's easy. We value the organization, that is easy. What is helpful is that to continue to strive and move the organization forward, we must look both ways, forward and reverse. Looking in the rearview mirror can show us the successes and challenges we have had. We need to study the past because much can be learned from it. The strive for success is constant and ongoing during your tenure as the leader, or even as an up-and-coming leader. We want to continue generating successes and minimizing the challenges. Such can help us pave the way for the future, make calculated decisions, make decisions that will get a buy-in from the critical infrastructure and take the organization to the next level.

Remember, there are no shortcuts to any place worth going...

ASKING FOR A FRIEND

I always enjoy reading a social media post where someone will pose a question that may be controversial, embarrassing or otherwise one that will likely by all accounts offend someone, so they say "...asking for a friend." Realizing this is a facade I put some stock in this concept and began applying it to leadership. You see, there are leaders out there who lack a spine, backbone, or the intestinal fortitude to be a leader. Unfortunate as it may seem, they do exist and hopefully we can fix this or learn how to deal with them.

We've spoken about free beer tomorrow, the square peg in the round hole and a host of other concepts you may find helpful toward your leadership quest. Great leaders need to have the moral courage (guts) to tackle things head-on. The "asking for a friend" syndrome is not an option. Skirting issues, blaming others, or not taking accountability is not a viable option. In fact, as said throughout, respect is earned, not taken. If you want to get respect you have to give it, not rocket science, right? Some leaders may not be able to approach people in a respectful manner and have that candid or difficult conversation. Remembering the golden rule of treating others as you want to be treated, there are many successful ways to approach these conversations without slamming your fist down on the desk or raising your voice.

One of the worst things a leader can do is lie. It's true, everyone tells a white lie here and there, and some more than others. As a leader, lying may give you temporary relief or help you avoid a contentious situation. Consider it good luck because you may have dodged a temporary bullet that was shot in the air. However, shoot a bullet straight up in the air. What happens next? It will fly high in the air but eventually it will come back down. Apply this same principle to lying, it may fly high and take off with great momentum but eventually it will lose its velocity and come back down. Lies can bite you in the ass and sometimes in a very painful fashion.

Leaders must be able to tackle the tough conversations, and no one said it is easy but with experience it becomes easier. I'd like to look at a couple of different approaches you may find helpful. First, if you are the person who enjoys having a tough conversation with your people, perhaps you should not be in a leadership position. Meaning, you should have the highest regard for your people and not look forward to having these conversations. Yes, I get it, life is easy, people make it hard. There are times when you want to smack someone with a rubber hose, especially people who go out of their way to piss you off or intentionally do something that may double your workload. However, people are still your critical infrastructure and will always be. As such, you should not look forward to these conversations nor seek enjoyment from them. Rather, look at these as a necessary evil and you must take it head-on.

I like to consider the "blame soft, praise loud" approach to difficult conversations. Before getting into that, we must look at how to approach the difficult ones. I have been asked this by up-and-coming leaders and have shared the same response each time. As leaders, we have tools in the tool chest. These tools perform a variety of tasks to help us fix things. But there is not one tool that fits every situation so it can be fixed. You have to select the proper tool and apply it. Sometimes you could be looking for a 9/16 socket and select a 3/8, 5/8 or 1/4 before you finally get the right one. The more you use the tools, the better you get when having to use them the next time. Apply this same principle to tough leadership conversations. You cannot grab one tool and hope that it will work right. You may get lucky the first time and grab the right socket and if so, it is good for you. However, there are times when you will have to methodically select the right one to do the job. By not using the tools and trying to unscrew something by hand may not get the job done. You must make the proper selection and when you do, it may make it quite easy.

Apply this same principle when speaking to others. As I said before, sometimes you must be the chameleon and change colors. Not skin colors, of course, but rather to be able to adapt to the person with whom you are speaking. You get to know your people and gain an understanding of their persona, and how they react to certain things. I had a supervisor who worked for me, and this individual had many fine qualities. However, it seemed like the only time they would listen is when they would get yelled at. No one likes to yell, and no one wants to be on the receiving end of yelling. This person was the exception to the rule but nonetheless that was what it took. In cases like this it may be best to try to get this person to conform without having to be yelled at. Cases like this are a bit of an outlier, but it happens. By the way, the person is no longer in a leadership position.

On the other hand, individuals have different means of accepting or receiving criticisms, advice or perhaps just getting simple orders. There is not a boilerplate model that works for everyone and in a perfect world the leader would give instructions or orders and others would just follow. However, we know that does not exist. So as a leader, you have to be able to adjust to your individual people. In turn, your people will adjust to you. It's a fair trade and can help you work in harmony to get things done. Regardless, you cannot perform the "asking for a friend" conversation to avoid taking things head-on. I like to call it a "firm but fair" philosophy where others know what to expect from you and you know what to expect from others. In the spirit of transparency this will bode well for you.

I recall a situation that happened one time when I was an up-and-coming leader. The person above me would make blanket statements, unfulfilled comments and over promised and under de-livered on promises. They would avoid the difficult conversations by referring to other people and the things they may have said, just to divert the difficult part from themselves and blame a third party who is not present. It was "...so & so said you need to be doing this." With "so & so" being a higher up in the organization. The reality was it was not "so & so" but it was them, they just didn't have the guts to say it was coming from them. It is always easy to speak for other people when they are not there, especially higher-ups, to bypass taking your own responsibility when having that difficult conversation with someone. If you are looking for ways to lose respect from others, this is a good means of doing so. Such can be even worse when the matter is dissected, and you discover the leader was not being honest with you. In fact, this is a guarantee that respect is right out the window.

No one said being a leader is easy and it can get lonely at the top sometimes. However, you cannot stick your head into the sand like an ostrich and hope that things around you will get better, or people will like you just because you are their leader. Face it, people may not ever like you. You will be blamed for a lot of things that are not under your control nor things you had anything to do with. Sure, there will be peaks and valleys, but you have to take the bad with the good and the good with the bad, that's how it goes. You simply must create as many peaks as you can and minimize the valleys. When you are in the valley, you may have someone throw you a lifeline but should not sit in the valley waiting for one. Rather, climb out yourself, learn from that which got you there and minimize the opportunity of going there again.

A young police officer I knew had a vibrant career ahead of him. He worked with us for a bit and then went to a larger agency. It seemed like a great opportunity to him to spread his wings and fly. He had so much potential, carried himself well and never quit smiling, three very good traits in my book. As time went by, some two years later, he stopped in to pay a visit. I wish it was just to say hello but that was not the case. Rather, it was the first time ever I did not see him smiling. I thought perhaps something had happened to him and became worried. When I saw him, he asked if he could talk to me, to which I gladly invited him into my office. I asked how the job was going and he said that was why he was there. He explained to me how unhappy he was in his new position. I thought to myself if anyone would succeed it would be him. He went on to say that his supervisors were lousy, and they would always say, "...upstairs is not going to be happy..." in referring to the chief and administration. Apparently, they were all housed upstairs somewhere. Clearly not high enough because the shit was trickling downhill.

His expressions were abundantly clear to me that he was very unhappy, and it all stemmed around the leadership. He explained some of the criminal cases he made, community policing initiatives he completed along with being a proactive police officer. He said he has been working hard but it was never enough. The supervisors are giving him the oldest police car, lousy assignments and critiquing everything he does. When he would ask them about it, he would receive the same response, " ...this is coming from upstairs..." Again, not far enough upstairs. I felt bad for him because the guy who never quit smiling had finally quit. In fact, he said he was considering quitting his job because of how unhappy he was.

I gave him a few pieces of advice, one of which was to see if he could schedule an appointment with "upstairs" and seek some better guidance. I realize this may not be altogether possible, but any chance is worth taking. Next, I recommended he get his marching orders in writing and then measure his accomplishments in writing so as not to get the "upstairs" lecture. We had a good conversation and it seemed to cheer him up a bit. I am glad he trusted me to seek help and it worked because he made some adjustments and is on track toward his first promotion.

In consideration of what he told me, I catalogued this into the "asking for a friend" syndrome. I say this because the supervisors were unable to tackle problems directly and had to push off blame to "upstairs" to avoid the tough conversation. It is easy to blame upstairs because these leaders probably hide behind a desk or, to the contrary, have no idea what their first line supervisors are saying. These may be very good leaders at the top echelon, but they need to get out and about. The leadership philosophy of leading why being out and about is not a new concept but rather one that has been around for a while. Are you the leader who is out and about or do you hide in your office and avoid everyone?

The situation of which I just spoke is unfortunately not all too uncommon. Therein, a very good officer was being tainted and tarnished because the supervisors he reported to were lacking a spine and blaming "upstairs." However, some of you may be thinking that maybe it was "upstairs" that was causing this. Perhaps such was the case, but if it was, then the mid-level managers should be stepping up and recognizing how a good employee was becoming cynical because of the upper leadership. This is the last thing we want to see happen in any organization.

Thinking more about the "asking for a friend" syndrome pushed me back to my early days when I worked for an iron fist supervisor. This supervisor would spend twice the effort in trying to get out of doing something than simply just doing it. The leadership style was by coercion, intimidation, or just being a dick, which he was good at. In fact, if there was a Guinness World Record for being the biggest asshole in the world, he would have been the clear winner with no distant second. I think you get the point.

The gist from this individual was the coined phrases he would use. For example, if he came to you in front of others and said, "Do you got a minute?" meant you were about to get your ass handed to you in one form or another. It was so bad that some others began using it too, which is bad juju. If you want to be an up-and-coming asshole, this was the way to do it. Another one was, "do you have something you want to tell me?" I wanted to say, "...yes, you are an asshole and I never want to be like you, ever..." but being the young officer, I would just say no and then wait for my lunch to be delivered by him or he'd grab the scissors and clip my wings for something miniscule just to make him feel important. When he finally retired, he was definitely not invited to his retirement party.

When I teach new supervisors, I give them a couple key words like "you got a minute" or "is there something you want to tell me." I usually get a laugh or two from the students because it seems like many entities have the buzz words that are the triggers that something is about to happen and it's probably not good. From the leader I mentioned in the paragraph above, his key phrase was, "Got a minute" and then game on. It did not settle well with many because you were about to get your ass handed to you on a silver platter. In many cases it was minor shit that he made into major shit simply because he was good at being a dick. This empowered him, made him feel superior and fueled his fire. However, what he failed to realize was that it was generating a huge amount of resentment. In fact, it is safe to see he was not well liked at all. When you are counting the days until someone retires, it is probably not because you want to make sure you give him/her a good retirement party. Rather, it is the polar opposite, you want to throw a banana at the door every time he walks by it. Think about it.

I have solicited the key words from others and have added them to the list and it keeps growing. Here are a few:

Hey, you got a minute?

Anything you want to tell me?

Step into my office

What message is it sending? The wrong one. We need to get away from this as leaders, break the mold and consider alternatives. Leaders need to understand the barriers these create. I understand, delivering or having unpleasant conversations is not desirable but rather a necessary evil. Again, looking forward to these is not something good leaders should do. Taking them head-on, of course, is necessary. However, for the 101st time, people are our infrastructure, and we need to value them, even when they screw up.

As I mentioned earlier, Johnboy's one piece of advice for future leaders: do not forget where you came from. If you did not like the "asking for a friend" syndrome or the buzzwords where you knew you were about to get your ass chewed, then make these go away. To this day, I make it clear to others, please do not ask me if I have a minute.

I will give you a blanket answer that I will always have a minute or will make a minute, just do not ask me that. Sounds crazy but these words can be impactful, and they need to be broken. The good news is you have the power to make them go away, so do it!

Don't ask for a friend, have the guts and grab the bull by the horns. Again, no one said having a leadership position is easy. Good leaders are needed and why can't it be you?

Let's carry on...

LEADERS: MADE OR BORN?

It is a realistic question to ask whether leaders are made or born. There are many debates to be had from both sides. Some may say that one was made to be a leader by the efforts put forth while others may say the person was born with certain traits to make them a successful leader. Regardless of your position on the debate, we should all be able to agree upon one thing and that being a leader is not easy.

That said, my argument would favor one who has worked to become a leader by using those inherent skills, attributes, personality, and general demeanor developed throughout life. If you are one expecting a silver platter to be handed to you, step in line and take a number as odds are you will be waiting for a while. I like to refer to the "wish in one hand and shit in the other, which weighs more?" philosophy. In other words, if you have the desire to be a leader, then pursue it. If others are identifying some of the leadership traits you possess, either they are kissing your ass for some reason or being honest in identifying your abilities. Hopefully it's the latter.

Born or made, something you should also ask yourself is why you want to be a leader. There could be many reasons but consider how genuine these are. If you are one who enjoys bossing people around, you should rethink leadership. If you are one who has been picked on your entire life and want to have the final say in things, then reconsider leadership. If you want to make a difference, impact, and help others, or otherwise make the world a better place, then you are on the right track. We need to be honest with ourselves and realize that some people are just not cut out to be leaders. Again, this does not make them bad people as most of them are still good people.

So, what approach does it take to be a good leader? There are tons of books out there telling us how to be one. I have read many of them and cannot think of one that I did not benefit from reading. I am hoping you will feel the same after reading this book. I found that the realistic approach to leadership is likely the most beneficial. There are some leaders who put themselves on a plateau or put on a good front for others. Such is not to be critical of them as they are probably good leaders. However, how they see themselves versus how others see them is entirely different. Take the leader who feels that everyone loves them but when he/she leaves the room and closes the door there are a few dozen darts hitting the closed door behind them. Having a realistic approach to leadership does not mean you have to make substantial changes but rather look through the lens of simplicity. Are you trying to fit the square peg into the round hole? Are you offering free beer tomorrow? Will people laugh at your jokes even though they put people to sleep? Will people come to your retirement party out of obligation or desire?

A realistic approach to leadership encompasses many traits. You do not put on a façade, you face issues head-on, you develop new leaders within the organization, and you appreciate people. This is not new but when is the last time you told someone "Good job" and meant it? Earlier we talked about blame and praise, treating others how you want to be treated and a host of other traits. Are you using these tools?

Let's take a good look at some of the key qualities a leader should possess, in no certain order:

As only a partial list of many of the qualities needed to be a leader, which of these do you possess? What would you add to this list? Whatever those are, do you also possess these traits?

Looking at the list, most of these are learned or acquired traits versus ones you are born with. Or some may argue that some may be inherent skills, like having a good personality, patience, or humility. Setting aside the question of whether leaders are made or born, the more important question is which of these skills do you have, and which of these do you need to work on. A good leader will strive to have all of these and more, knowing full well these could be fluid at times.

When it comes to people skills, I often get asked what the best way is to administer discipline when it is necessary. First, it is never easy, nor fun, enjoyable, or uplifting. It can be difficult, frustrating and impact you outside of work. If it doesn't then perhaps you may need to reevaluate because this should not be enjoyable, nor should you look forward to these situations. As I shared previously, I like the blame soft and praise loud approach. While employees may have broke policy or perhaps did something to get them into trouble, they still must have some good qualities about them. Consider accentuating the positive traits to boost them up versus beating them down.

As we examine effective listening and communication, this one can be tricky because it takes effort. Listening and hearing are not the same and we need to be able to identify this. Communicating and speaking are also not the same which we also need to identify. How much effort do you put into listening to someone? Our thought speed works much faster than our speech speed and often when we are talking our mind can race ahead. Or, when you are listening to someone you are too busy thinking about what you are going to say next versus listening to what the other person is telling you.

Next, honesty, integrity, and passion, all three are very good qualities. Most would argue these are traits developed over a lifetime and always developing. A good leader must be honest, even when it comes to tough times. As I mentioned earlier, lying may give temporary relief or may help avoid a challenging situation. But again, like shooting a bullet into the air, its going to come back down. If you are not honest your people will know. The trust they have in you will be broken and you just cancelled your ticket to your retirement party. Honesty goes along with integrity and how you hold yourself. Do you hold yourself to a higher standard? In doing so, do you remember that everyone puts on their shoes the same way? Remember the plateau analogy. You are not to be standing up there all alone, you need to be bringing people up with you. You need to do the right thing even when no one is looking, and I'm certain you have heard that before. It is an easy trek to go on but it is also an easy trek to sway from. By holding yourself accountable and being honest will also bolster your integrity.

In several locations in this book, I have mentioned moral courage. Simply put, a person with moral courage is one who has guts. As I have remarked many times, being a leader is not easy. However, it will only be as good as the effort you put into it. Having moral courage is a tremendous asset. It is an acquired trait and develops more and more over time. We must be careful not to confuse moral courage and confidence because, while similar, they are not the same. Some leaders' heads can become quite large to the point they are over-confident and stepping on the toes of others. They may feel untouchable, boisterous, cocky, and will not be invited to their retirement party. Leaders whose heads get too big will likely fail, unfortunately. I do not like to look at it this way but give some thought to some of the leaders who have failed and the reasons why they did. I'm betting that one reason may be that they got too big for their britches, and no one brought them back down to earth. They may fit the mold of a bosshole and a shortage of friends. If one is in this position, maybe they will have the moral courage to ground themselves and change into the leader they once were. While optimal, it may be difficult but will be worth it in the end.

Moral courage can be synonymous to standing up for others and occasionally means sticking your neck out. It is acceptable to stick your neck out but just be careful that it is not too far. Knowing your limits is helpful and those who you stand up for will have more stock in your leadership. I know you are waiting for an example so here you go. Ohio has a statute that makes it a crime to knowingly file a false complaint against a peace officer. Today's police officers are subjected to many challenges and need to be on their best behavior always. With technology and the ability to record the actions of others and post onto social media, it can be harmful when officers make mistakes, despite them being human. As a police chief, I told our officers that if anyone ever filed a false complaint against them that I would sign the charges and arrest the person. These are only words, and they are only as good as the nature and spirit behind them. A person of honor and integrity will live up to their words and their promises. We all know how an empty promise is received and those on the receiving end can be hurt by them. While a criminal complaint of this nature is not common, it is there for a reason. Fast forward to a situation where a narcissist person actually filed a false complaint against one of our officers. I took on the investigation myself, gathered all the evidence and found it was a clear-cut violation of the statute. I lived up to my word and filed charges against the individual who still felt they did nothing wrong. We took it one step further and when the person was taken into custody, we used the handcuff of the officer with whom they filed the complaint. Make no mistake, police officers are imperfect beings just like everyone else. They are held to a higher standard than civilians and are subjected to many things an ordinary person is not subjected to. There have been unfortunately many cases where police officers break the law and are arrested. Sad but it has happened. However, a police officer should not be subjected to false allegations and those who do so need to be held accountable, just like officers need to be held accountable for their actions. I sought no praise or recognition for handling the investigation and filing charges, rather, I went above and beyond because I said I would. Imagine the outcome if I had dealt the case off to another investigator. How would the victim officer feel? I know how I would feel and it would be lousy.

There are many books, studies, research, and publications on ethics, and we all know what they are. I do not want to spend a lot of time on this topic because you should already know this by now. Many of the topics we have discussed in this book lead back to being ethical. There are far too many examples of when this was not the case, and these can be damaging to an organization when a leader goes down due to a violation of the code of ethics. I will say this about ethics: practice ethical behavior always. Do the right thing, think before you act and speak.

Lastly, a leader must be open-minded and practice humility. Leaders do not go into their respective positions to seek notoriety, recognition, or to be popular. Anyone who does this is not a good leader. In terms of being open-minded, I like to refer to a quote from Ken Blanchard who said, "None of us are as smart as all of us." The newest,

youngest employee may have little longevity but may also have a great
idea. A good leader is one who should listen to others, seek input from
others and allow others to have a voice. Obviously, this will depend
on the size of the organization but regardless of size, there should be
a mechanism to allow others to have a voice. A leader who is not
open-minded may overlook a key opportunity to better the organization. The leader may also miss recognizing an up-and-coming leader
by not lending others credence and an opportunity to contribute.

THE NO EXCUSE ZONE

O pinions are like assholes, everyone has one. The same can be said about excuses, everyone has one. The big question is this: what is your excuse? Rhetorical of course, but let's apply this in a couple different ways. First, if you are holding back from jumping into a leadership position, what is your excuse? If you are uncertain about your next move into that spot, why are you holding back? Or, if you are already in that leadership position, is there anything that is holding you back? Or, are you not running on all eight cylinders to keep the ship moving? If so, why not?

As a leader you will encounter many excuses for many things from employees. Why a certain assignment was not completed will be blamed on something. Why an employee was late for work or, worse yet, didn't show up for work but will have an excuse. Or, why a task was not carried out will be blamed on something else, etc. I think you get the point. I want to dedicate this chapter to getting your people on track and avoiding all the excuses.

Everyone is different as we know, and their capabilities vary from one to another. A good leader must realize that their leadership team may have commonalities in their leadership style, but they will not be your clone. Your expectations may be high as are theirs, but they may also be different in terms of the approach. All the same, you should all have the same goal in mind which is the betterment of the organization. The way you get there varies but if you are moving forward then you will be in good shape. There will be setbacks along the way, which are to be expected, but you should be prepared for these and ready to overcome them.

As it relates to the no excuse zone, this can be cultivated within the organization, like the key buzz words we spoke of earlier, such as "got a minute." I remember my early days as a young police officer. From time to time there would be a piece of equipment that would come up missing. Everyone would be blaming others then suddenly one day that piece of equipment would show up in the magic drawer. No one knew now it got there, but all the same, it was no longer missing. Yes, of course, the culprit was afraid to face the music or didn't want to get in trouble and somehow the item magically reappeared. It was not magic but rather culture. The hazing would have been relentless if they had fessed up and was more than they wanted if they had simply owned it. This leads us into the no excuse zone.

Is your organization so tightly wound up that employees will go to extremes to avoid fessing up, even if it would get them into more trouble than it would if they would have owned it in the first place? Herein, all roads lead back to the culture of the organization. Are the employees wound so tight that they are afraid to come forward because they made a mistake? You ask yourself, is he going to share an example and the answer is a clear yes.

A vibrant young police officer had fulfilled his dream of joining the agency where he lived and in doing so he had so much potential. He was bright, talented and had so many things going for him. I was so happy for him, and it feels good watching others work hard to get what they want. Unfortunately, it did not last all too long. You see, some of the culture called for minor picking on the new people, but it was not all that bad. It was part of the growing process and something we had all been through to some degree. It was not hazing, intimidating or otherwise a version of Paris Island. Rather, it was grooming the new people to have thick skin. I am not a proponent of hazing the new people, it does not bode well at all with me. Rather, new people should be accepted into the family of the organization and supported accordingly. However, in this case, the FNG, which stands for the effing new guy, thought his pride was too strong to break which became his demise.

Working one busy night, he was dispatched to a large fight amongst a bunch of drunk people which is a a priority. He arrived and helped others and the situation was resolved without incident. The next day, someone spotted damage to the police cruiser he was driving and reported it, which is standard protocol. The young officer said he must have hit it with his lawnmower at his house which would have explained the damage. However, the explanation did not match up to the damage. Rather than saying the truth that he struck something while responding to a hot call, he thought that excuse was better than the truth. Two words: bad idea. Instead of owning his mistake, he went to extremes to defend his lie. I wanted to throw a lifeline to him but by the time I was able to, the ship had already taken on way too much water and was about to sink.

The young officer was given an opportunity to save face, own it, put it behind him and move forward. Unfortunately, that was not the case. Rather, he dug in his heels and tried to justify certain things and then took to sharing purported transgressions of others to try to minimize what he did. Again, bad idea. It was a shame because this young officer had a lot of potential but blew it. It was his demise, and he was done, gone, game over. Sadly, he was let go. I was not the leader of the agency and essentially stayed out of things but, like everyone, had an opinion. I really wish he would have come forward, owned his shit, taken his lumps and moved onward. I was disappointed because I tried to mentor young officers, but this became a Jekyll-Hyde situation where his true colors came out, but I asked myself if the culture of the organization had a contribution. Such is not to say it did because I believe it did not, but it also bodes to ask leaders about the organization and how it handles certain situations. Does the organization ostracize others when they screw up? Or, do you allow them a chance to save face? It is unfair to blame the organization, but you should understand that the culture can impact employees and modify their behaviors. For example, if the water cooler talk is about bad mouthing the person who isn't there, we need to avoid it. I understand people are people and this will never go away. However, can we at least work to minimize this? Some leaders are guilty of the same behaviors and as shit slides downhill so do these actions. If the leader is bad mouthing or making fun of them behind their back, what do you think the subordinate personnel are going to do? You cannot sustain a "do what I say, not what I do" environment. Doing so will only cause short, medium and potentially long-term problems that are hard to overcome. It will also take away your ticked to your retirement party.

My recommendation is to avoid the no excuse zone. Do not let the organization develop one because you create an unnecessary risk of employees backing themselves into corners or situations that they cannot recover from. If I have not said it enough already and hopefully you are not getting sick of it, people are your critical infrastructure, and we need to value them. If you encounter a situation like that which I just shared, a good leader will ask him/herself if he/she contributed to it. Clearly in this case the officer made poor choices and essentially compounded it to the point of no return. It would be unfair to blame the administration for the actions of the officers, but it does bode to ask if there is a culture that pushes personnel into situations where they would sacrifice their careers just to avoid hazing. Or, in other words, they would cut off their noses to spite their face.

Many of us know this, but the road to hell is paved with good intentions. Wish in one hand and shit in the other, which one weighs more? A leader may have the best intention in the world but if your employees are going to extremes like this then perhaps it is time to press the reset button, reevaluate things and bring everyone together. The situation I shared is clearly not the fault of the administration. It was a shame, but the young officer was thrown many olive branches to rectify the situation but failed to capitalize on it. Again, it is a shame that he threw away a career and I feel badly about it. However, by the same token, there is a learning opportunity and that is to avoid the "no excuse zone" and it is perfectly acceptable to hold yourself accountable. Raise the white flag, you effed up, let's move on.

In terms of policing, here's another analogy. Policing and its policies need to be fluid. As a young police officer, if you would have told me that my future would include a policy that prohibited police officers from engaging in high speed vehicular pursuits, I would have laughed you out of the room. However, today, many agencies have policies that prohibit police officers from pursuing vehicles unless a certain criterion has been met. Like many organizations, mine developed such a policy where officers could not pursue vehicles unless it was a violent felony, or a person suspected of driving while intoxicated. Mostly narrow, it kept officers from chasing stolen cars and other violations where otherwise would have warranted them pulling out

the stops. I didn't like it, the officers didn't like it but it was a sign of
the times that was called for.

As bad guys became aware of this policy, there were many that
capitalized on it and decided to run from the police. It made the
situation difficult because we teach officers to catch the bad guys but
now, we have strings attached to it. You should go after the bad guys
but only in certain situations, otherwise let them go. Hello? Talk
about compromising your principles, this is to the fullest degree.

Fast forward a year into the policy where we had two police officers
violate the policy in the same weekend. While a policy may be fluid
in nature, they are also etched in stone. You either complied with the
policy or you did not. This is kind of like fitting the square peg into the
round hole. I had the chance to speak with both officers. One officer
came in, raised his hand, and said, "I effed up, my fault, won't happen
again, just got caught up in the moment." The other officer came in
and gave a plethora of excuses of what-ifs and a line of bullshit that
would make your blue eyes turn brown. Rather than holding himself
accountable, he chose the blame-shift-deny approach which did not
bode well for him. If you make a mistake, own it. Do not blame
others or try to fit the square peg into the round hole. The outcome
is not likely going to be good and ultimately may test one's degree
of integrity as it relates to the ability to hold oneself accountable.
Leaders understand that people will make mistakes but in a situation
like this, two similar situations and two opposite responses. What can
be gleaned from this? One officer held himself accountable, the other
didn't. Could it be maturity, training, policy or just their personality.
Either way, I would prefer the one who holds themselves accountable
and moves on. Belaboring a situation does no justice for anyone so in
most situations it is best to handle it and move on.

The situation bodes to ask, are your people holding themselves accountable? Are you holding yourself accountable? Do you offer a platform that allows people the opportunity to come clean without going to extremes? Unfortunately, situations like this can and do happen. The last thing we want to do is lose a good employee over a situation that is solvable. In today's world and at the time of this writing, good employees are hard to find. They are equally hard to replace if they decide to jump ship and seek greener pastures elsewhere. Such is not to say we should start letting the tail wag the dog because that could be no further from the truth. However, it does rise to the level of accountability where we need to do all we can to retain employees, invest in them as this is an investment in the organization.

We are making progress, one chapter to go!

LEAVE IT ALL OUT ON THE FIELD...

W ell, we are here, the last chapter. Throughout this book I have shared many analogies, stories and perspectives on leadership and related topics. Starting with the New York Yankees and Manager Joe Torre example, we saw how putting the right people into the right places at the right time can yield a very favorable outcome. I also shared several times the quote from my high school football coach who stated that wish in one hand and shit in another, which weighs more?

I mentioned several times the words moral courage in hopes you have a better understanding of the words but moreover it elevated your thinking to the point where you have the guts to be a great leader, but you will also keep it in check and not allow it to inflate your head.

There are many examples of failed leaders but more examples of successful leaders. You will encounter setbacks, challenges, peaks, and valleys. How you react to and overcome these will define you. Adversity strikes everyone, some harder than others. The ability to adapt and overcome adversity is paramount and will define you. As a leader you want to be impactful while at the same time knowing, honoring, and respecting your people.

Several dozen times throughout this book I spoke of the critical infrastructure of an organization, that being – of course – its people. The reason why I put so much emphasis on this is because many times this concept is forgotten. It does not matter the type of organization or its size, people make the world go around and we need them. Your people should be recognized as an asset and not a liability. Not everyone will fit in and there is no perfect utopia out there where things will be hunky dory. Getting the right people on board is important to any organization, keeping them on board it equally important.

I remarked on how the tail should not wag the dog and we cannot lose sight of this concept. We want to treat our employees well but in doing so we cannot give away the farm. There must be compromise from all sides to make progress. I mentioned several times about leaders who dig in their heels. There are likely going to be times when this will happen. Before doing so, consider the alternatives and changing your mind or reversing a decision does not make you a bad leader. It makes you a good leader because you are not afraid of reversing things and recognizing the decision may not have been aligned with best practice.

In looking into the future, consider what it holds for you as a leader or up-and-coming leader. In a perfect world we would have a crystal ball and could forecast things, prevent problems before they happen and bring about harmony in our organizations. Unfortunately, such crystal balls do not exist. You will have to rely upon studying the past to plan and predict the future. In doing so, enjoy the process but also crave the goal of achieving greatness. A good leader will constantly strive for greatness and shine along the way. Great leaders require great sacrifice to carry the organization to the next level. Failure is not an option, success is.

In a sports analogy, leaving it all on the field really makes sense for leaders. You give it your all 110% of the time and leave it all on the field. Be impactful. Embrace opportunity. Seek out others who will share a common vision with you. Seek out others who are better than you, stronger than you and will help you carry the torch. Be better, be best, be yourself. Maintain your confidence but keep it in check. You can do it, find a way to greatness. Find a way to be the best leader you can possibly be. Your people need you and you need them. Together, the world can be a better place.

Thanks for reading my book.

ABOUT THE AUTHOR

Author John T. Majoy is a chief of police with over three decades of experience in law enforcement. In addition to his law enforcement duties, he is an adjunct professor of criminal justice at Bowling Green State University and Tiffin University. Majoy has served in his current capacity and also that of an undercover agent, uniformed officer, narcotics canine officer, special response team officer and advisory board member. He also serves on several committees dedicated to the instruction and betterment of law enforcement.

Chief Majoy has also dedicated himself to missing persons as a key highlight to his career. Having worked many missing persons cases, Majoy went on to chair the Northeast Ohio AMBER Alert Committee for many years. He also served as the President of the Board of Directors for Cleveland Missing, an organization dedicated to helping families who have missing, abducted, or exploited loved ones.

Majoy has been recognized by the United States Attorney General for Outstanding Contributions to Community Partnerships for Public Safety and the Ohio Association of Chiefs of Police, Certified Law Enforcement Executive, 2022 winner of the Dr. Ray A. Miller

Alumni Leadership Award for Outstanding Contributions to Law Enforcement

Having worked for good and bad leaders, Majoy has taken his career, experiences, peaks and valleys, along with his isms to compile a unique look at leadership through his lens in hopes of making himself and others better leaders.

ACKNOWLEDGEMENTS

It was always a bucket list item for me to write a book. Having never done this before, I had to rely upon others for guidance, direction, and insight. While it always was in the back of my mind on what I would write about and that which I would like to share, it was not until a life changing event that led me to start writing. Most chapters came easy as it seemed more like a reflection than anything else. I have learned a lot about myself through this process and know that I have much more to learn in my journey. I would like to thank my family for their support in me writing this and my daughter who designed the cover.

Like any good leader, you are only as good as those who you surround yourself with. Unfortunately, sometimes leaders are surrounded with people who will always agree with them or otherwise not tell them certain things in fear of hurting their feelings or otherwise upsetting them. Herein, I would like to personally thank Ann Meredith, Edward Yates, Dr. J. Christopher Mariotti, Tracy McGinley, and Jennifer Osborne. All are friends and colleagues who took time from their busy schedules but moreover time from their family to help me complete this book. I will be forever grateful.

www.ingramcontent.com/pod-product-compliance
Lightning Source LLC
Chambersburg PA
CBHW060247030426
42335CB00014B/1618